AWESOME ART PHILIPPINES

10 works from the country of 7,000 islands that everyone should know

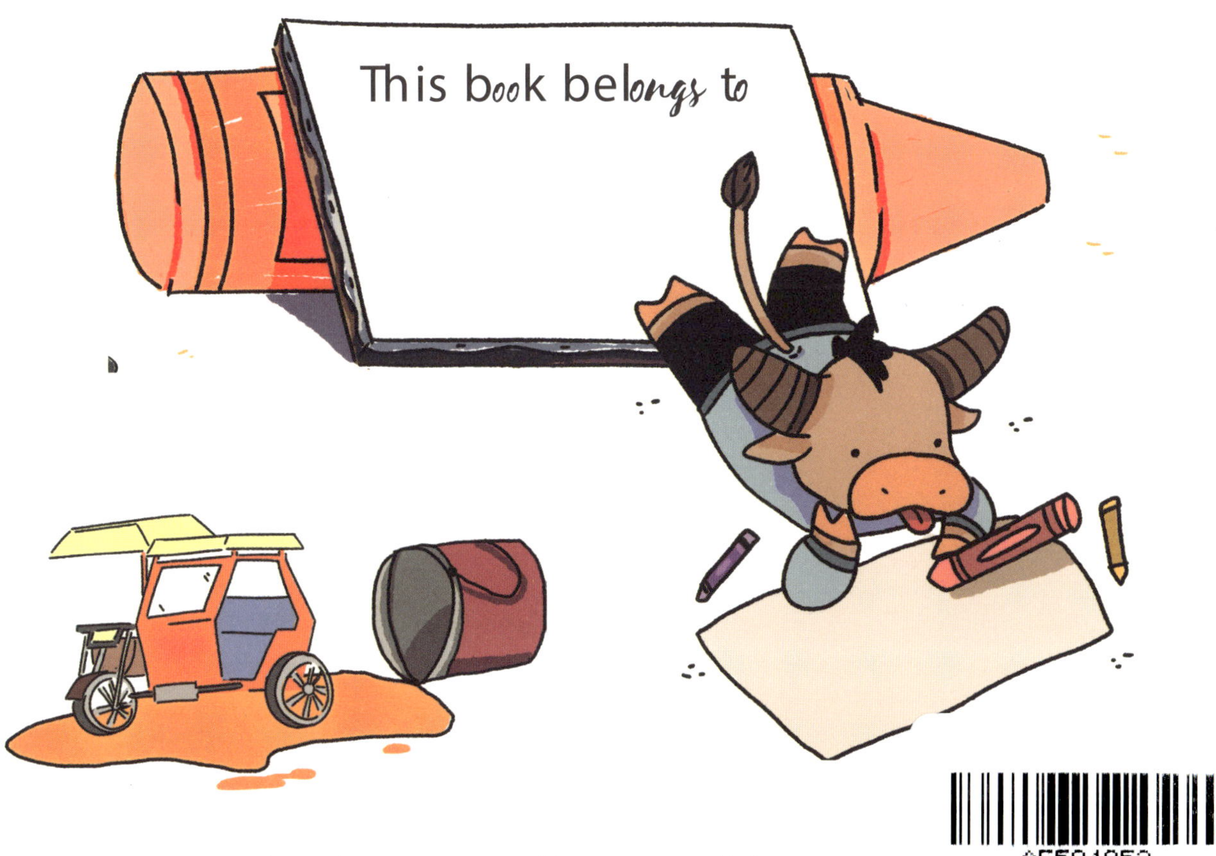

by Norma Olizon Chikiamco

Welcome to the Philippines! I'm Cardo the carabao, here to show you around this archipelago of over 7,000 islands.

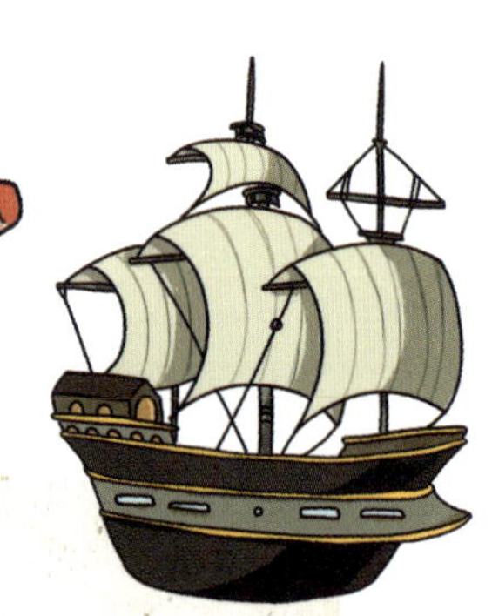

Because the Philippines is surrounded by nothing but water, it was easy conquest for invaders sailing from the West. In 1521, the Portuguese explorer Ferdinand Magellan landed in the Philippines. Because his voyage was paid for by Spain, the Spaniards laid claim to the land for 350 very, very long years. Spaniards influenced every aspect of Philippine life: education, culture, language, religion and the arts.

Although the Philippines won its independence in 1898, Spain still treated it as its colony. But then, a new coloniser arrived: the United States of America (the USA). After a mock battle, Spain secretly handed the Philippines to the USA for 20 million dollars! Over the next 50 years, American culture seeped into the Philippines. However, World War II brought its own colonisers to the islands, when they were invaded by the Japanese. With the end of the war in 1945 and the defeat of the Japanese, the Philippines was liberated with help from USA and its independence was finally recognised in 1946.

Now that we're caught up on the history of the Philippines, let's explore the visual arts of this incredible archipelago together!

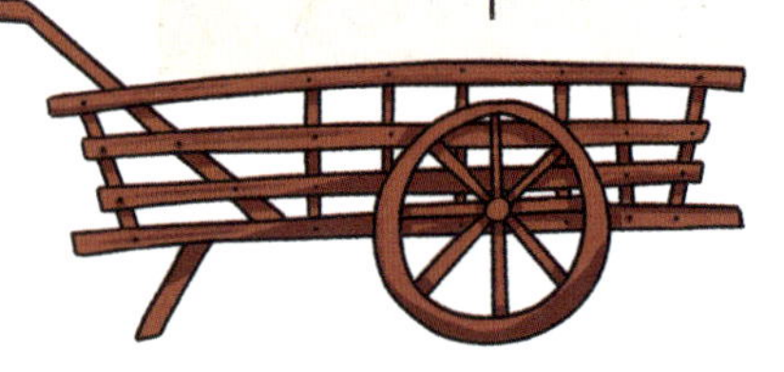

ESPAÑA Y FILIPINAS (1884)

BY JUAN LUNA

In *España y Filipinas*, the artist Juan Luna portrays a familiar closeness between the two countries: the coloniser (Spain) and the colonised (the Philippines).

Both ladies have upswept hairdos crowned with laurel wreaths, wearing dresses like those from ancient Greece. The lady on the left is Spain. She has a lighter skin tone, brown hair, is taller and has a mantilla on her left arm. Her right arm is wrapped around the waist of the lady on the right, who symbolises the Philippines. She has a darker skin tone, black hair and is shorter. Spain's arm seems to be stirring the Philippines toward a certain direction. This may imply the tight hold Spain had on the Philippines - like she was the boss!

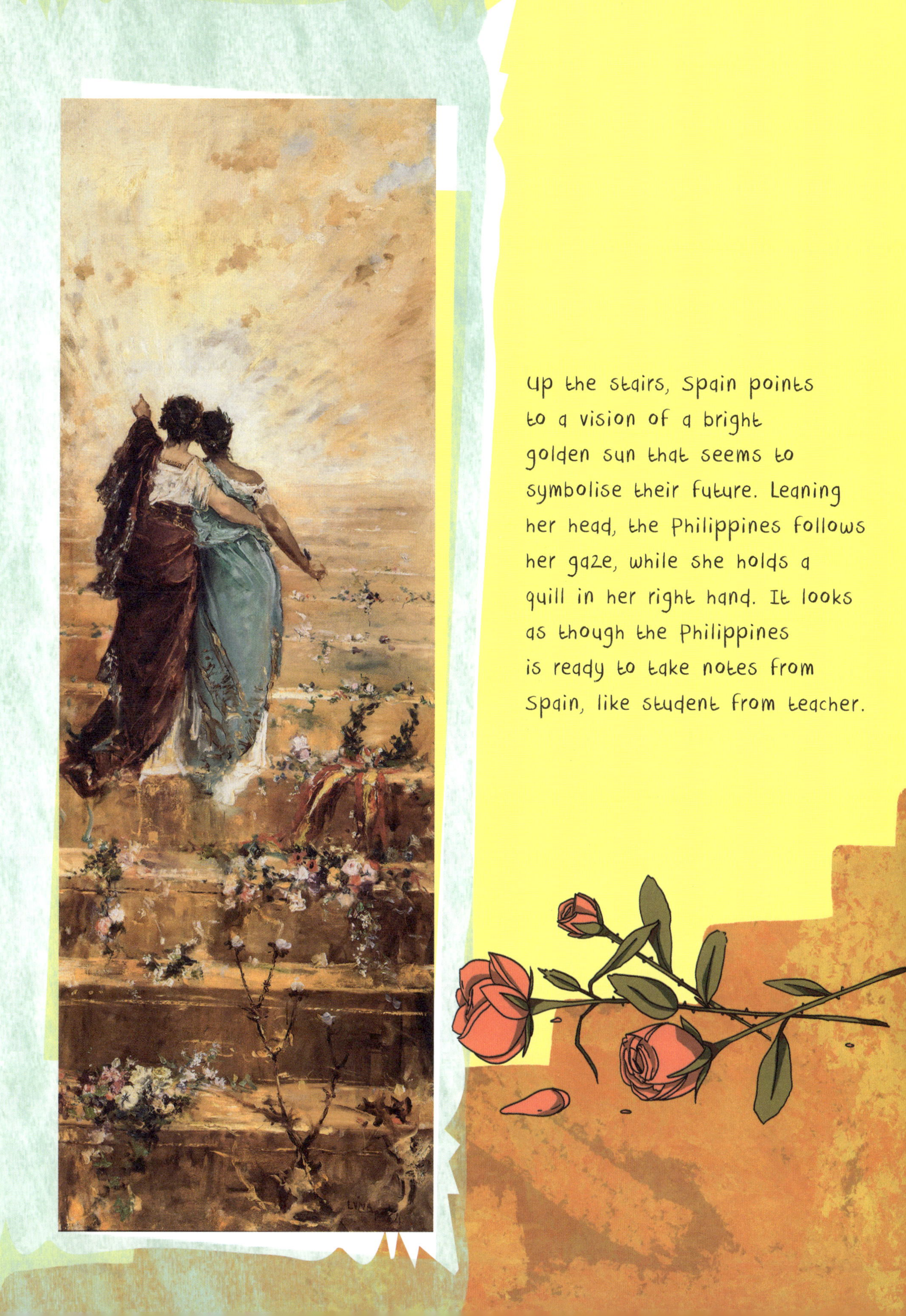

Up the stairs, Spain points to a vision of a bright golden sun that seems to symbolise their future. Leaning her head, the Philippines follows her gaze, while she holds a quill in her right hand. It looks as though the Philippines is ready to take notes from Spain, like student from teacher.

THE RED AND GOLD SASH ON THE STAIRS SEEMS TO REPRESENT THE COLOURS OF THE SPANISH FLAG. CAN YOU FIND THE COLOURS OF THE PHILIPPINE FLAG? IN FACT, THE PHILIPPINES WAS NOT YET AN INDEPENDENT NATION AND DID NOT HAVE ITS OWN FLAG!

The steps they have ascended are strewn with flowers, as if they had come from a path that blossomed with sweetness. However, a few of the stems have thorns! Perhaps Mr Luna wanted to imply that there was sweetness, as well as pain and sadness in their journey. This type of painting is known as allegorical painting, as the work uses symbols to convey an idea.

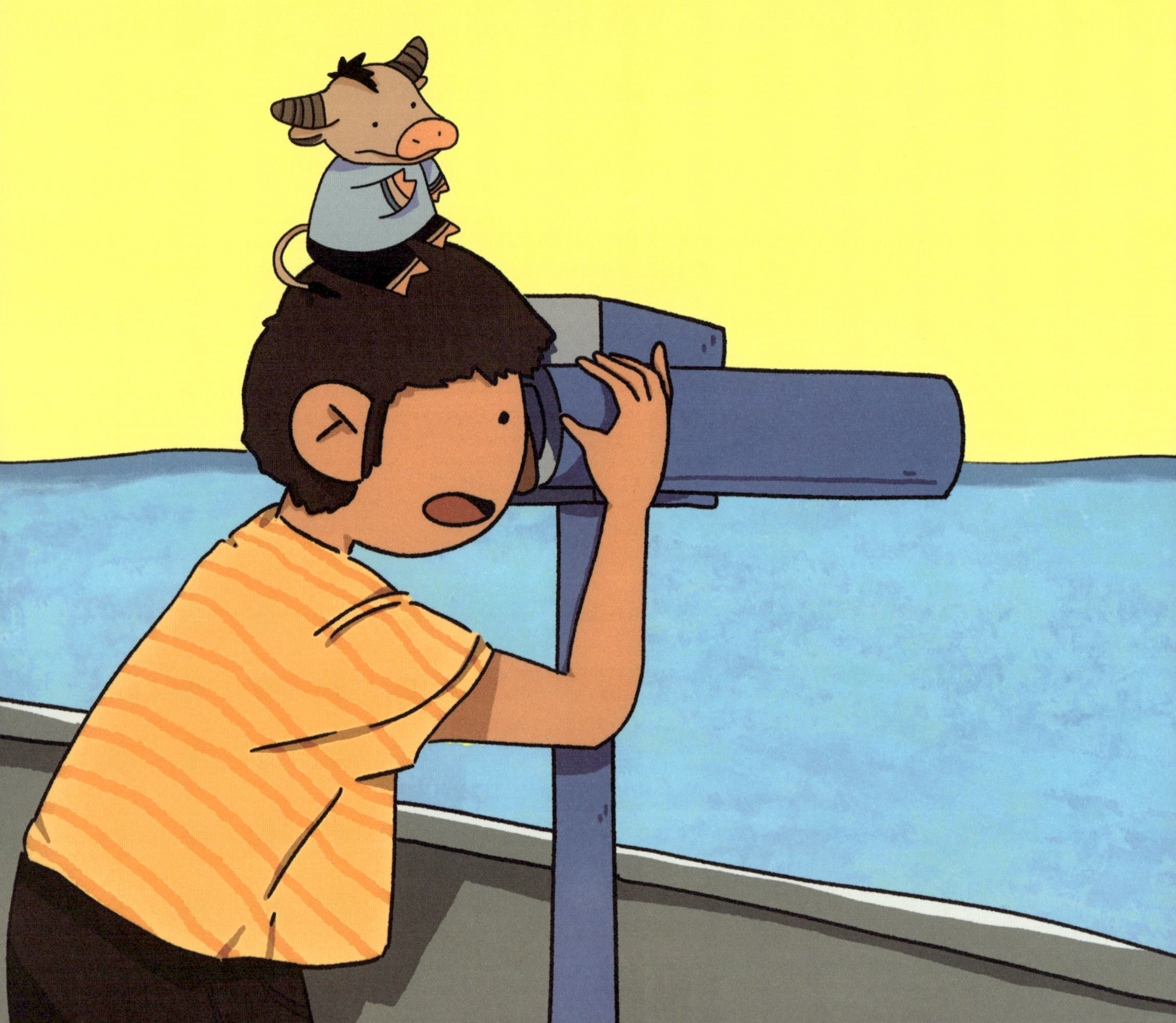

A VOYAGE OF DISCOVERY

Juan Luna was born on 24 October 1857 in northern Philippines. Though he longed to take up painting, he instead enrolled at the Nautical Academy - not because he loved the sea, but to get his parents used to the idea of him being far away.

Although his parents initially objected to Mr Luna becoming a painter, they later sent him to Europe to study art. He found inspiration there and garnered much acclaim, even winning top medals at national exhibitions of fine arts in Spain in the early 1880s!

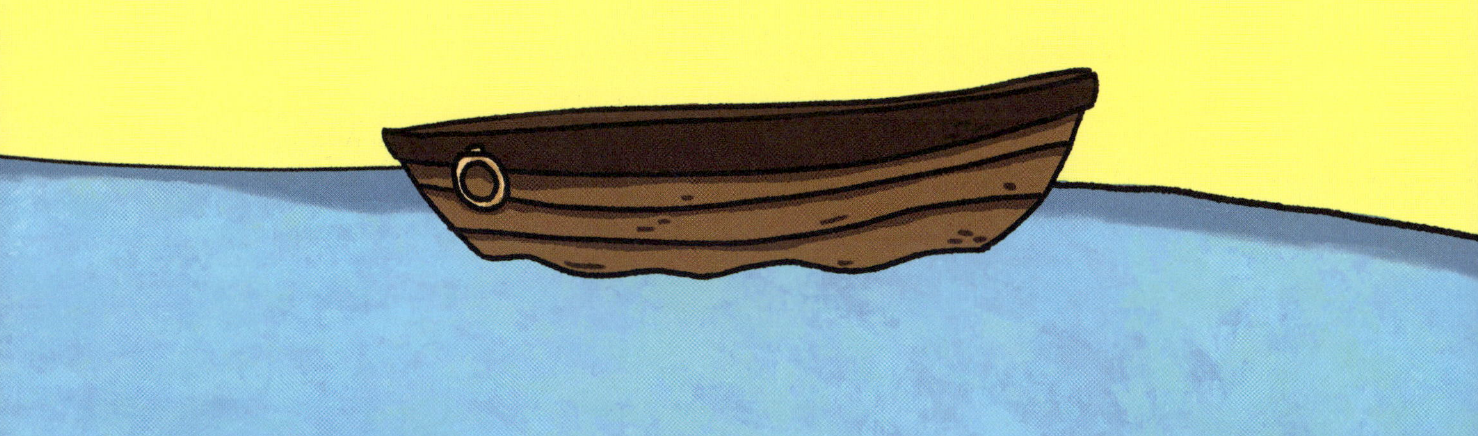

ANALYSING ALLEGORY

An allegory uses characters, objects, or events to symbolise an idea. Here, Mr Luna has used two ladies to represent the historical relationship between Spain and the Philippines.

Can you think of other historical events that can be represented allegorically? What characters or objects could this be represented by? Why do you think an artist might paint allegorically?

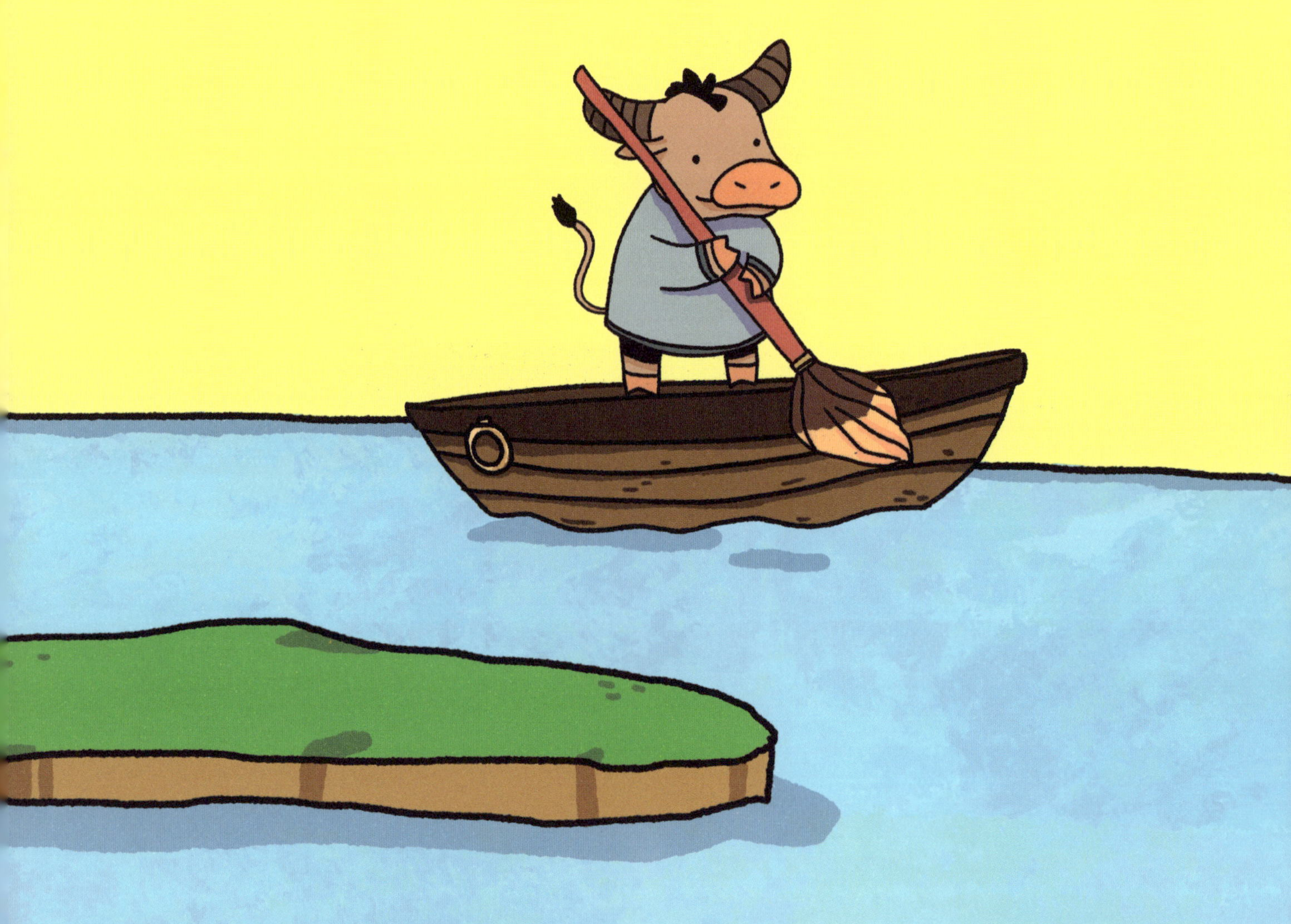

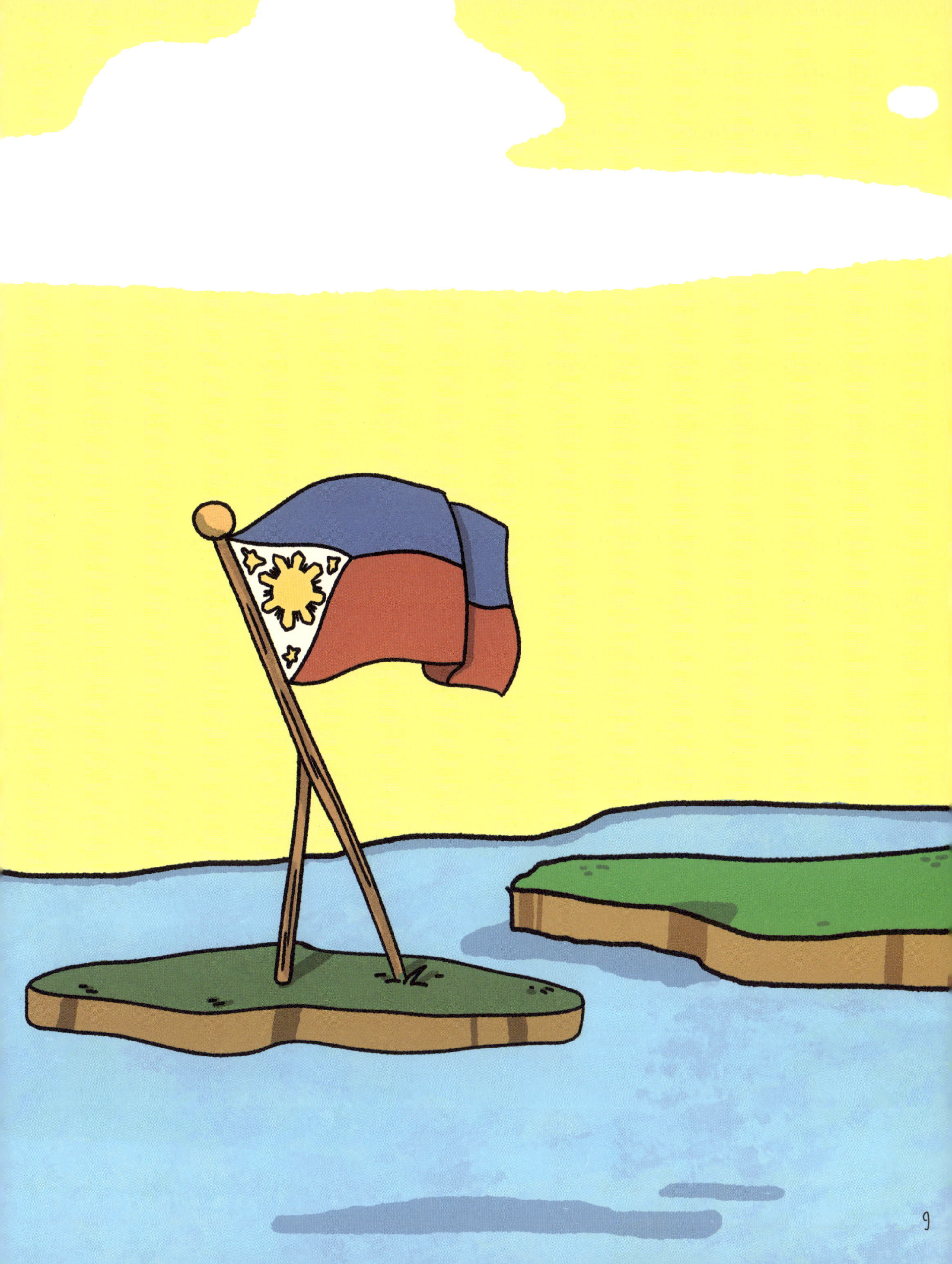

PORTRAIT OF JOSE RIZAL (1902)

BY FABIAN DE LA ROSA

This is a formal portrait of Jose Rizal, the Philippines's national hero. It was copied by Fabian de la Rosa from an earlier portrait of Mr Rizal done by fellow Philippine artist Juan Luna (p.4-9). At that time, it was common practice for artists to copy works of art which they admired.

In this portrait, Mr de la Rosa uses light and shadow to create contrast between the subject and the background. Against a dark background, you can see how the light falls on Mr Rizal's right side. Darker still is the background against which he is painted, so his figure stands out. This also makes the painting look more three-dimensional and life-like. This technique of using light and shadow is known as *chiaroscuro*.

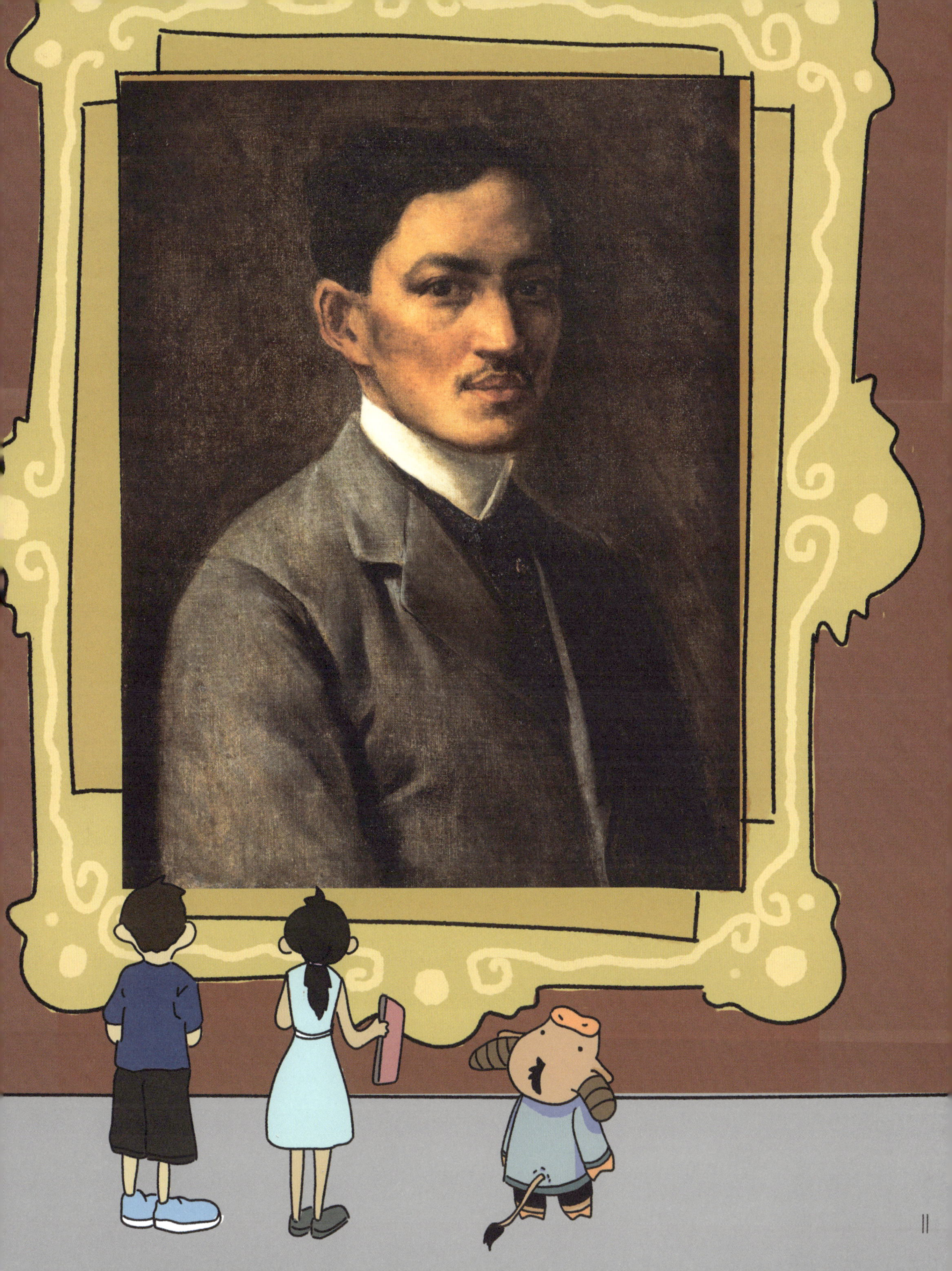

WHO IS JOSE RIZAL?

Jose Rizal, the Philippines's national hero, was born on 19 June 1861. He was a child prodigy who learned to read and write at an early age. Later, he became an artist, writer, sportsman and physician. Above all, he was a nationalist with a deep love for his country. He believed Filipinos and Spaniards should be equal, a belief the Spanish government was unhappy with. They accused Mr Rizal of taking part in a rebellion against Spain and executed him on 30 December 1896, in Bagumbayan. A monument to him still stands in that place, now known as Rizal Park.

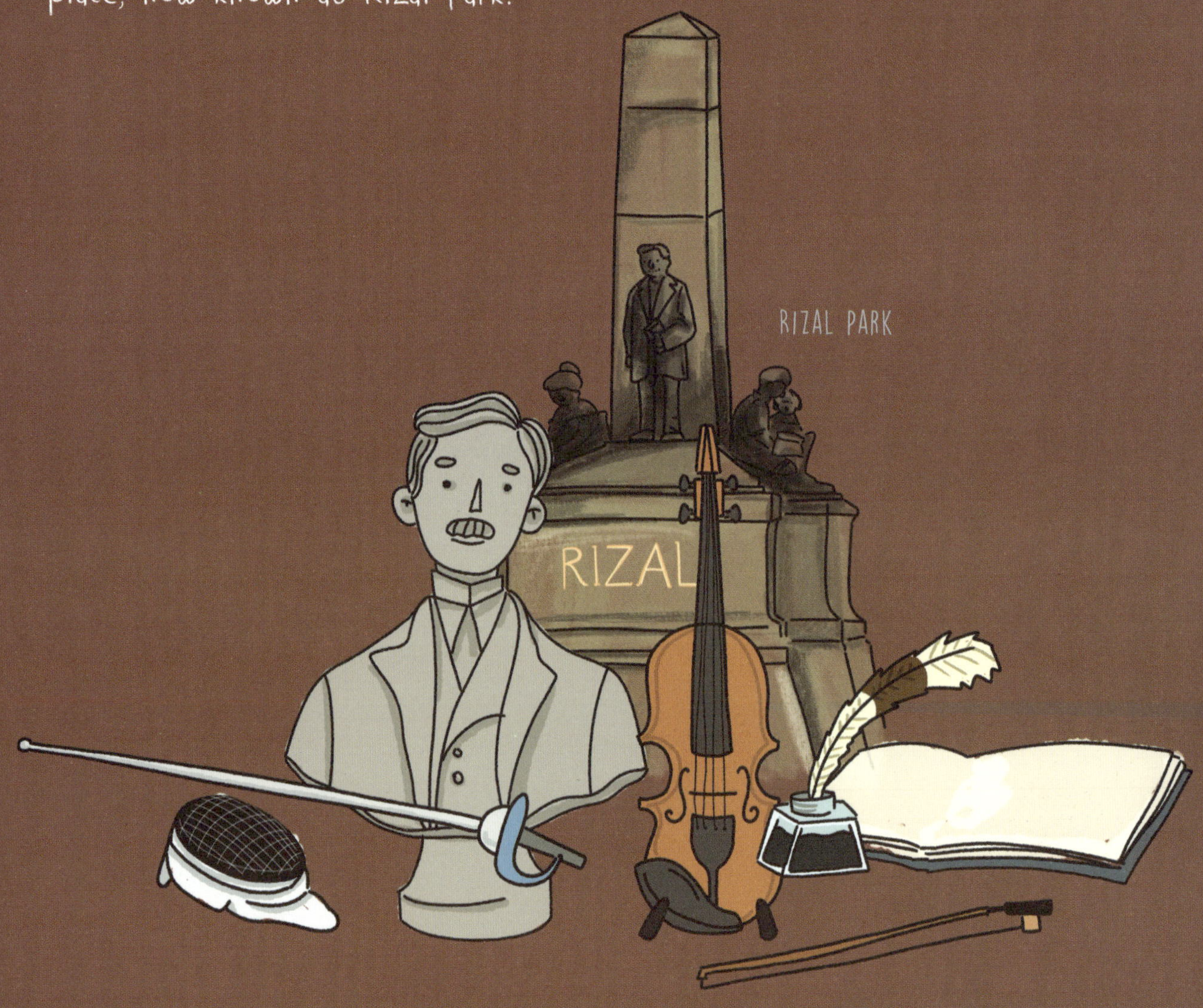

MR DE LA ROSA AND HIS PICTURE-PERFECT PAINTINGS

Born on 5 May 1869, Fabian de la Rosa received early training from his uncle, the painter Simon Flores y de la Rosa. Mr de la Rosa was also the nephew of painter Mariana de la Rosa and the uncle of renowned Filipino painter Fernando Amorsolo. Art was in his blood.

Mr de la Rosa lived during two colonial periods - the Spanish and the American - and witnessed many events significant to the history of the Philippines. Yet his paintings did not reflect these struggles. Instead, he painted landscapes, scenes of ordinary life as well as portraits of prominent people like former President of the Philippines Manuel L. Quezon and the 28TH President of the United States of America, Woodrow Wilson. Why do you think Mr de la Rosa created such paintings instead of historical ones?

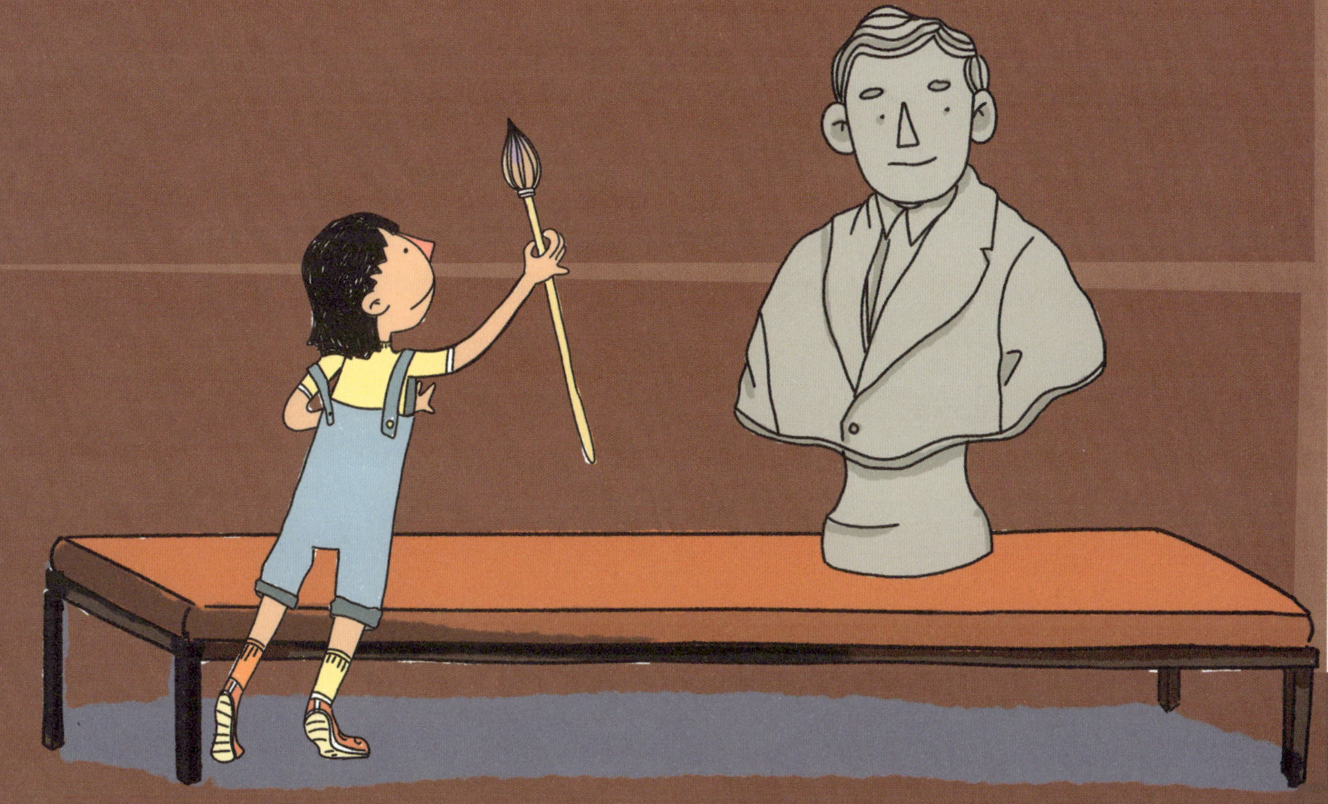

CREATING CHIAROSCURO

Can you see the difference in these illustrations of the painting by Mr de la Rosa? Darker areas are created by using deeper, more intense colours like black or brown. Areas in the light are much brighter and use the same colours mixed with white.

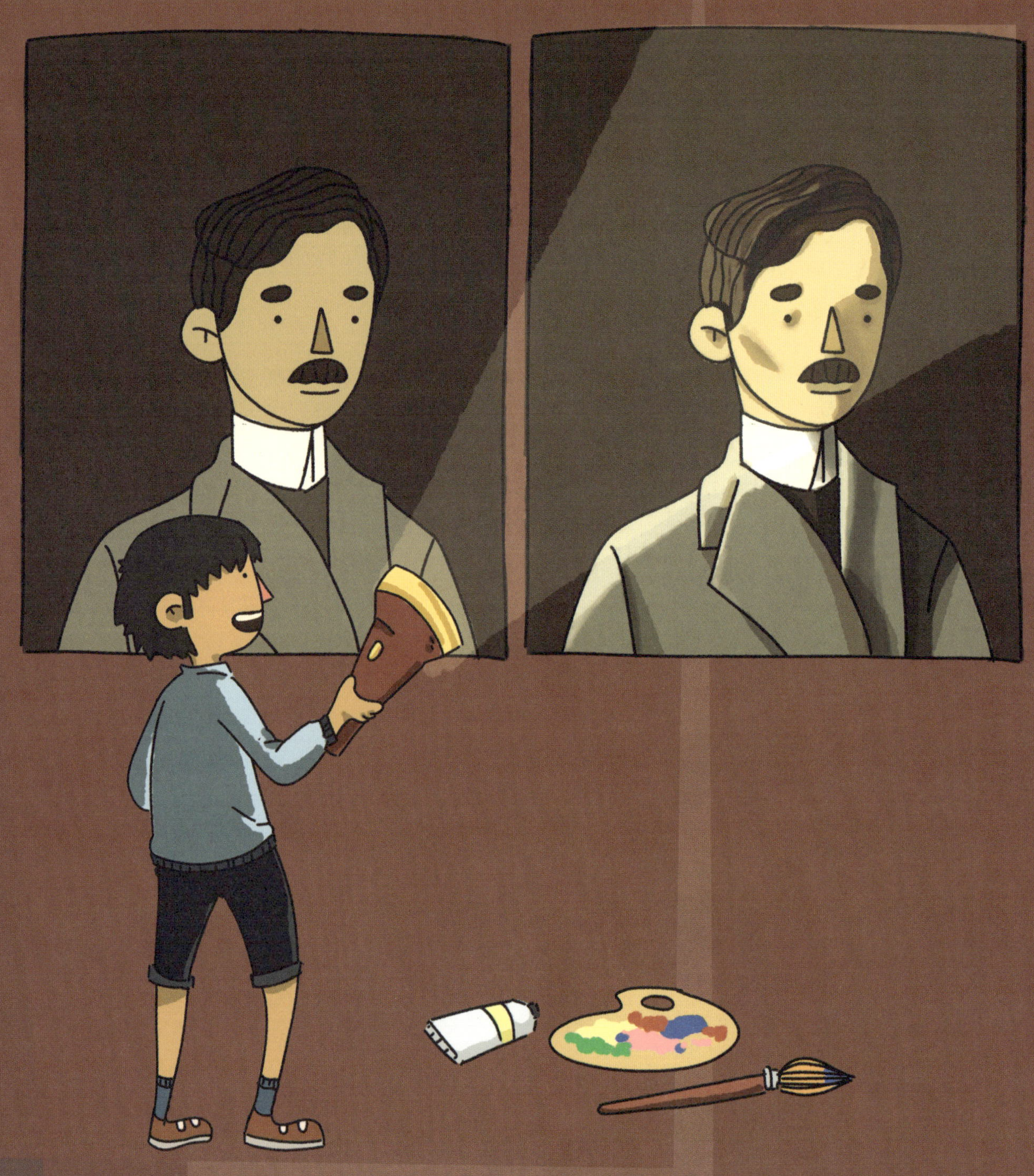

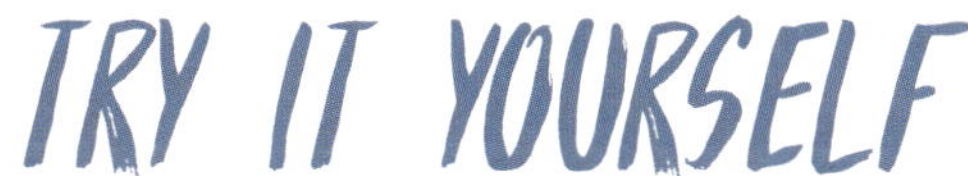

Using colour pencils, create chiaroscuro on the vase.

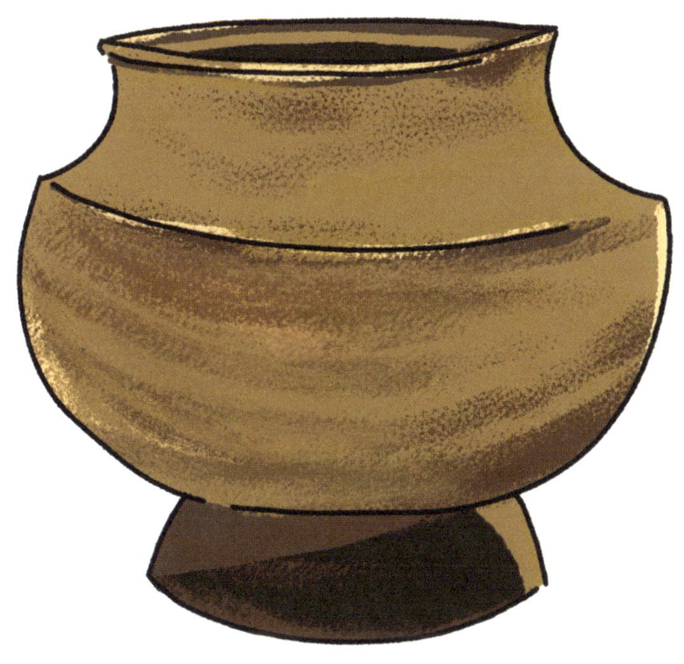

GIVE US THIS DAY (C.1974)

BY RICARTE PURUGANAN

In this chaotic scene, Ricarte Puruganan depicts a whole range of human emotions during the Japanese occupation of the Philippines in World War II. There is fear, panic, sadness, bewilderment and desperation to stay alive. Do you think the painting looks dynamic? That's because of all the action in it!

Notice a uniformed figure on the left, weapon in hand, chasing two men carrying heavy sacks on their shoulders. Another such scene plays out behind them, while in front, a figure cringes in fear or shock as a young boy stretches his hand for food. Two other ladies wrap their arms protectively around their children.

What do you think is happening in this painting? Mr Puruganan likely intended this painting not just as a criticism of the Japanese soldiers, depicted in uniform, but also of some Filipinos who collaborated with them. According to the artist's family, the original painting was destroyed during the bombing of Manila towards the end of the war. Mr Puruganan recreated it in what may be a larger format, seen here.

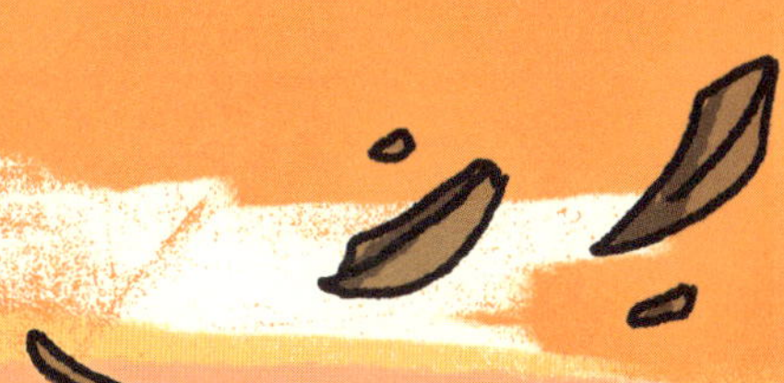

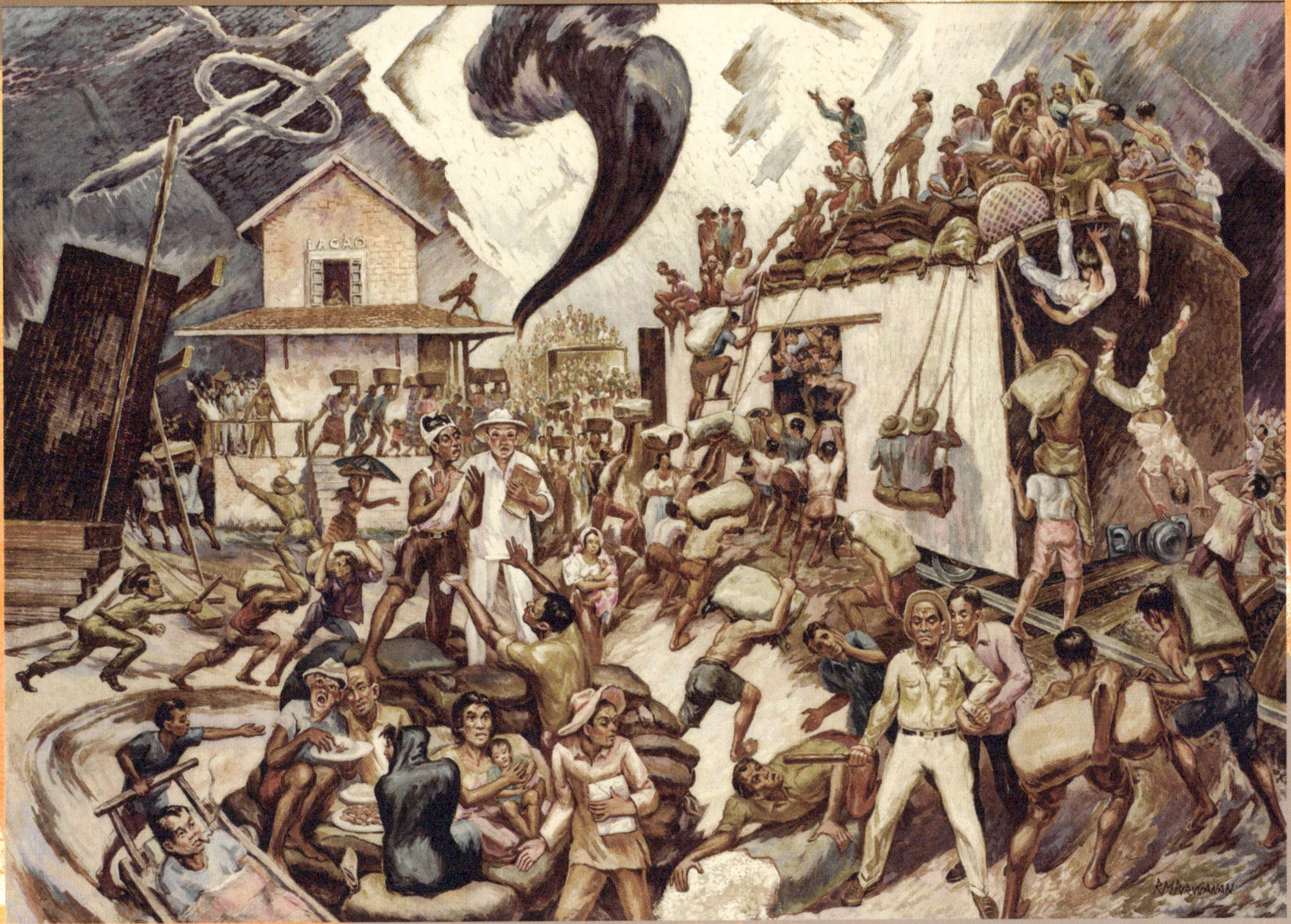

FACIAL EXPRESSIONS ARE ONE WAY BY WHICH ARTISTS EXPRESS THEIR SUBJECT'S EMOTIONS. HOW ELSE HAS MR PURUGANAN SHOWN THE EMOTIONS OF THE PEOPLE IN THIS PAINTING?

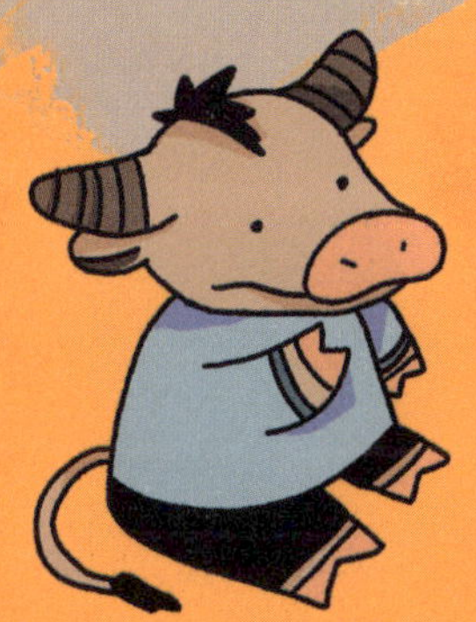

THE LIFE OF RICARTE PURUGANAN

Born on 20 November 1912 in Dingras, Ilocos Norte, Mr Puruganan at first wanted to be a musician like his father Honorio. But as a young man, he showed exceptional talent in the visual arts. Eventually, Mr Puruganan became a painter, and won awards and distinctions for the works he created.

THE *TINIKLING* IS A FILIPINO FOLK DANCE USING BAMBOO POLES. DO YOU HAVE A FAVOURITE DANCE?

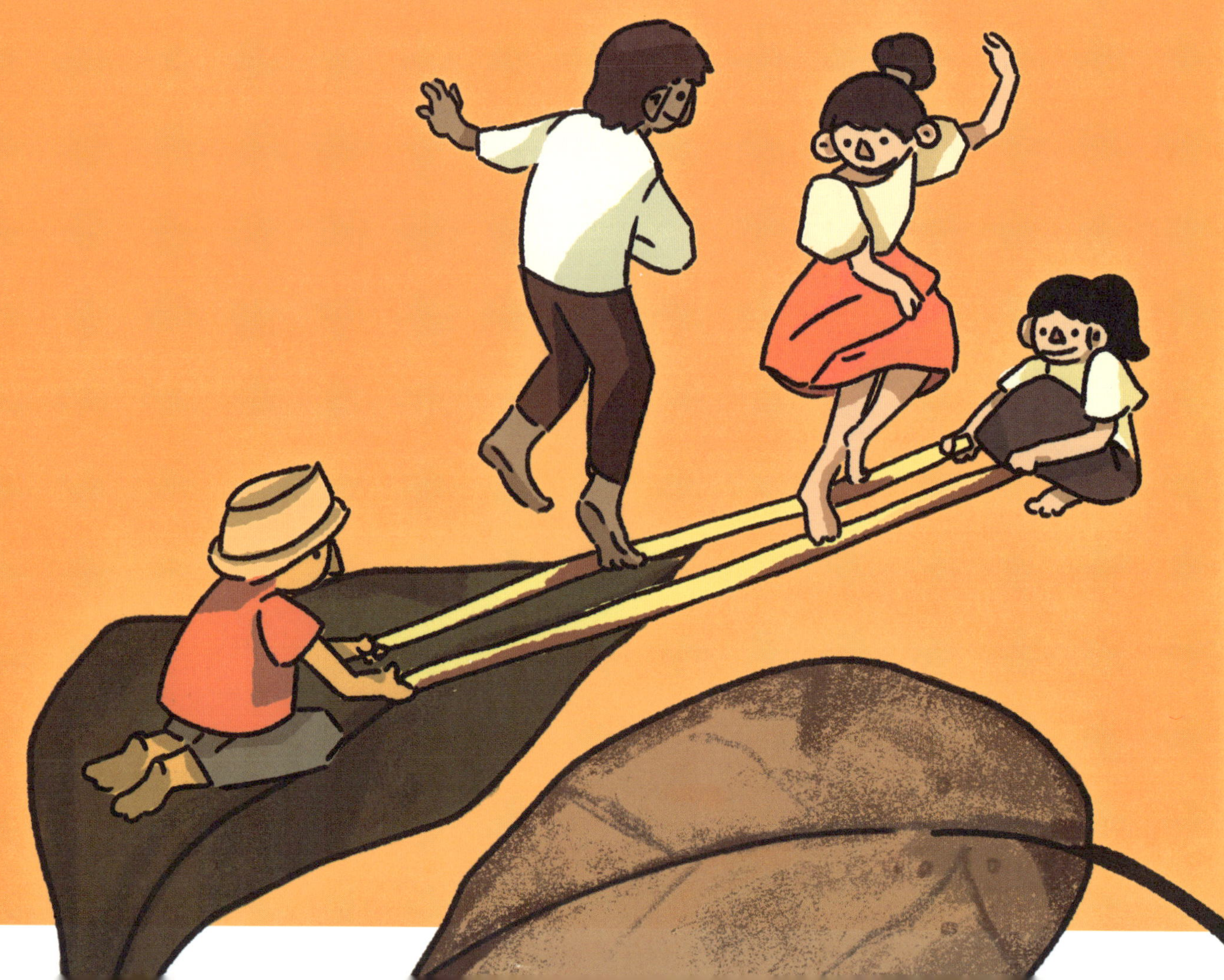

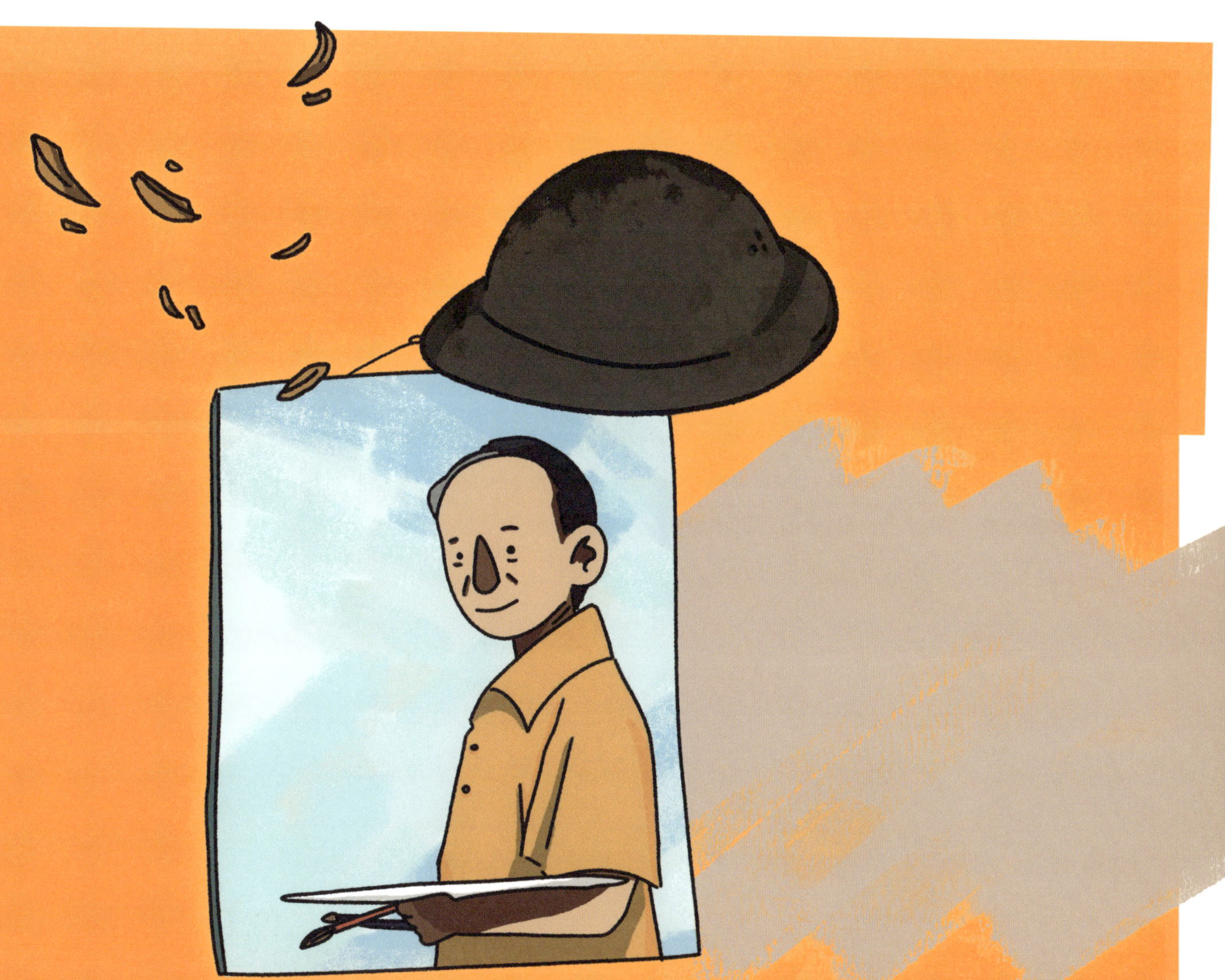

Many of Mr Puruganan's early paintings depicted the horrors of war. Two such paintings were finalists in the National Art Contest but they were disqualified by the Japanese-run government for being anti-Japanese.

For a period after World War II, people feared Mr Puruganan had been killed. In fact, he was alive and had just stopped painting to join the real estate business. When he started painting again, his works were more optimistic, with bright colours and happy subject matter. He also researched Filipino folk dances and art extensively, even writing a book about it. Many of his paintings in this period were also inspired by this. Later in his life, Mr Puruganan helped design and construct public and private buildings, including the Provincial Capitol in Laoag City.

PAINTING FROM NATURE

Mr Puruganan used many earth colours in this painting. Earth colours are those found in nature, like dirty brown, verdant leaves and warm shades of sunny yellow. You can create earth tones by combining the primary colours blue, red and yellow all together. A little more red paint creates an orange-brown, while more blue makes a colder shade! Grab some paint and mix up your own earth colours!

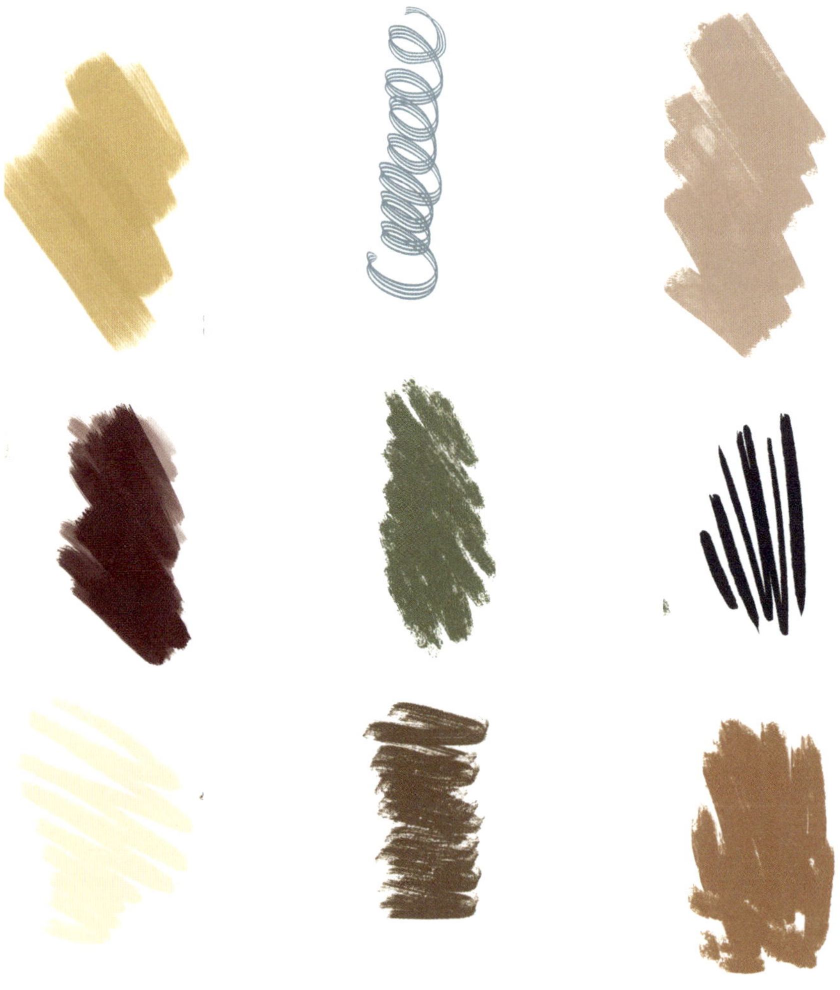

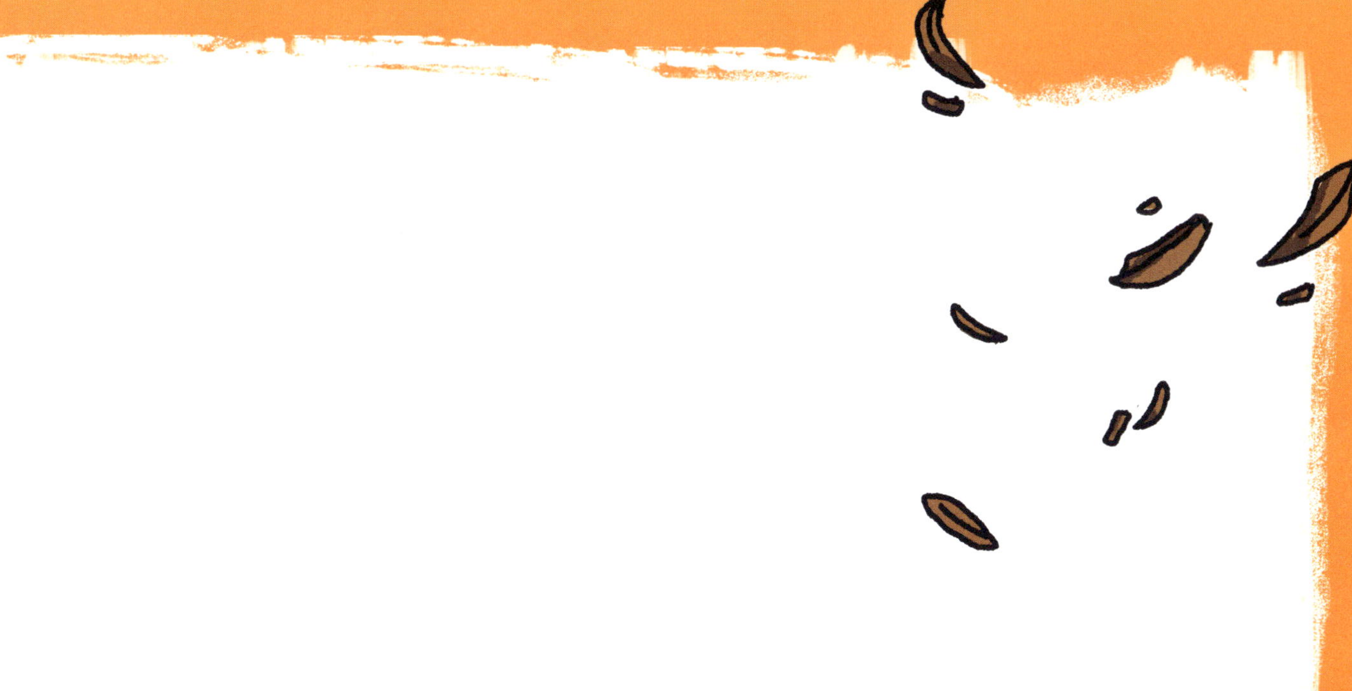

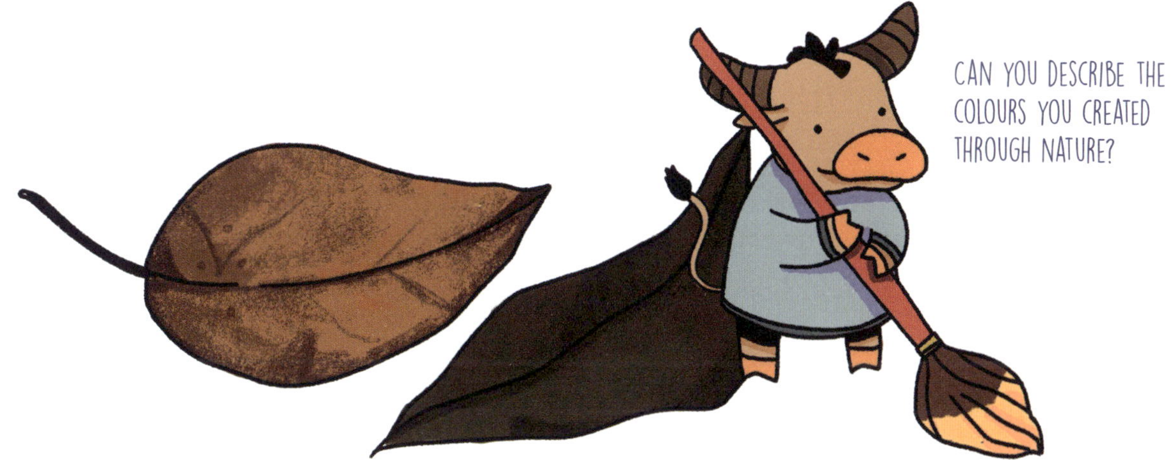

CAN YOU DESCRIBE THE COLOURS YOU CREATED THROUGH NATURE?

MGA NINUNO VIII (ANCESTORS VIII) (1976)

BY IMELDA CAJIPE ENDAYA

This is part of Imelda Cajipe Endaya's *Ninuno* series. In Tagalog, *ninuno* means "forefathers." Ms Endaya was inspired to create this series by her exploration of Filipino identity and ancestry. But what is Filipino identity?

Ms Endaya came upon the Boxer Codex, a book about people in the Philippines during the 16TH century. She found images of how they looked and dressed. From these images, she adapted two of the figures in this work, depicting them in grey. Next to them, she included four orange figures that are strikingly different. Depicted in much less detail, they look more like silhouettes and shadows. Why do you think Ms Endaya did this? Let's look at the rest of the work for clues.

In the background of this work is a reproduction of a document called *Doctrina Christiana*. The *Doctrina Christiana* was one of the first books printed in the Philippines. It contains the teachings of the Catholic church. The *Doctrina Christiana* shaped the identity of Filipinos' forefathers. However, might it also have erased other parts of their identity? Maybe that's why the orange figures look ghostly and elusive.

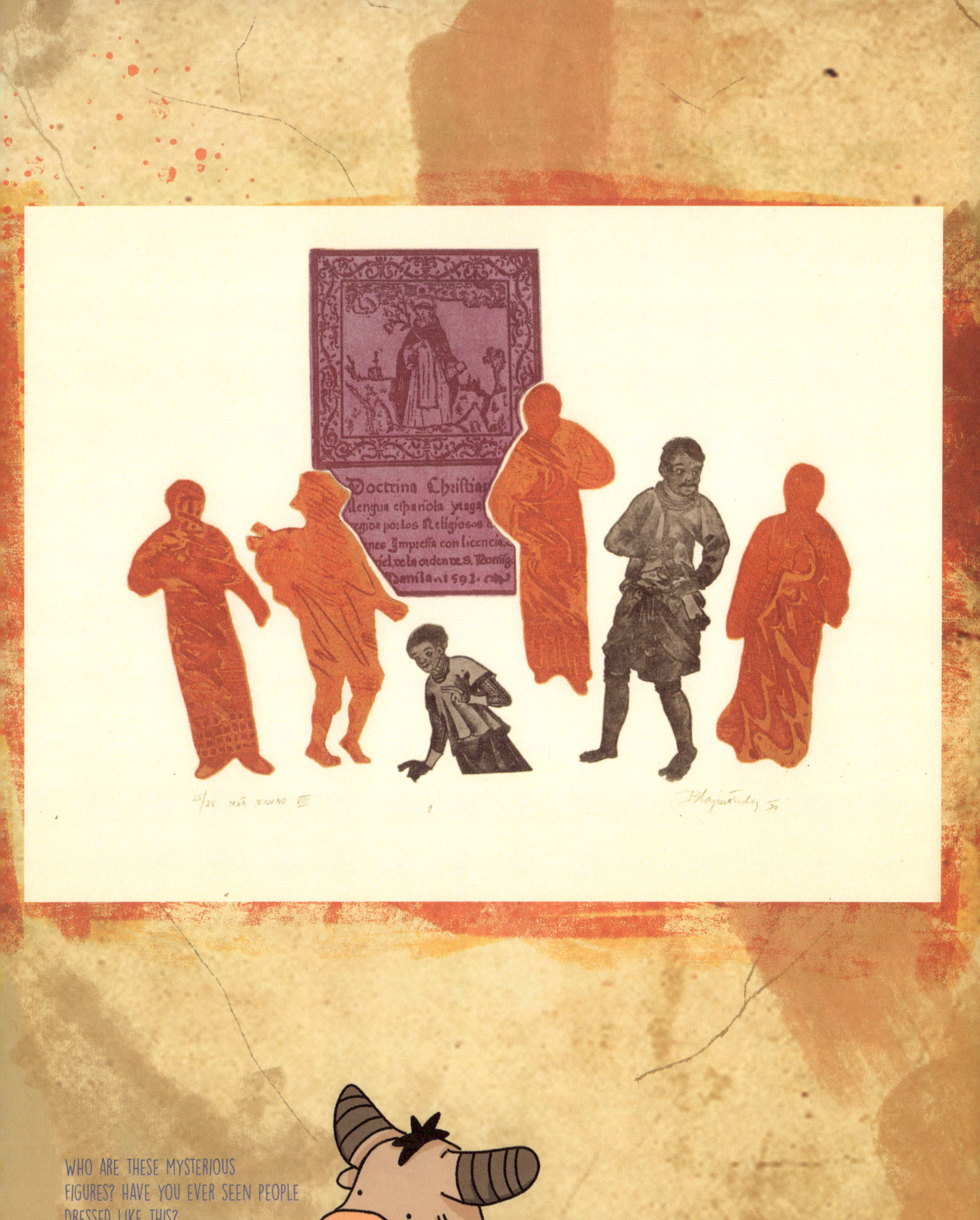

WHO ARE THESE MYSTERIOUS FIGURES? HAVE YOU EVER SEEN PEOPLE DRESSED LIKE THIS?

IMELDA CAJIPE ENDAYA'S MIXED MEDIA

Imelda Cajipe Endaya started as a printmaker, with etchings, calligraphy and serigraphs among her early works. In 1979, she was awarded a gold medal in printmaking by the Art Association of the Philippines.

Ms Endaya later shifted to oil painting. She has also created installations and mixed media assemblages where she used indigenous materials such as sawali, capiz shells, and found objects like ribbons and candy containers. Many of her works delve on themes of national identity, human rights, political, social and feminist issues, as well as the plight of migrant workers.

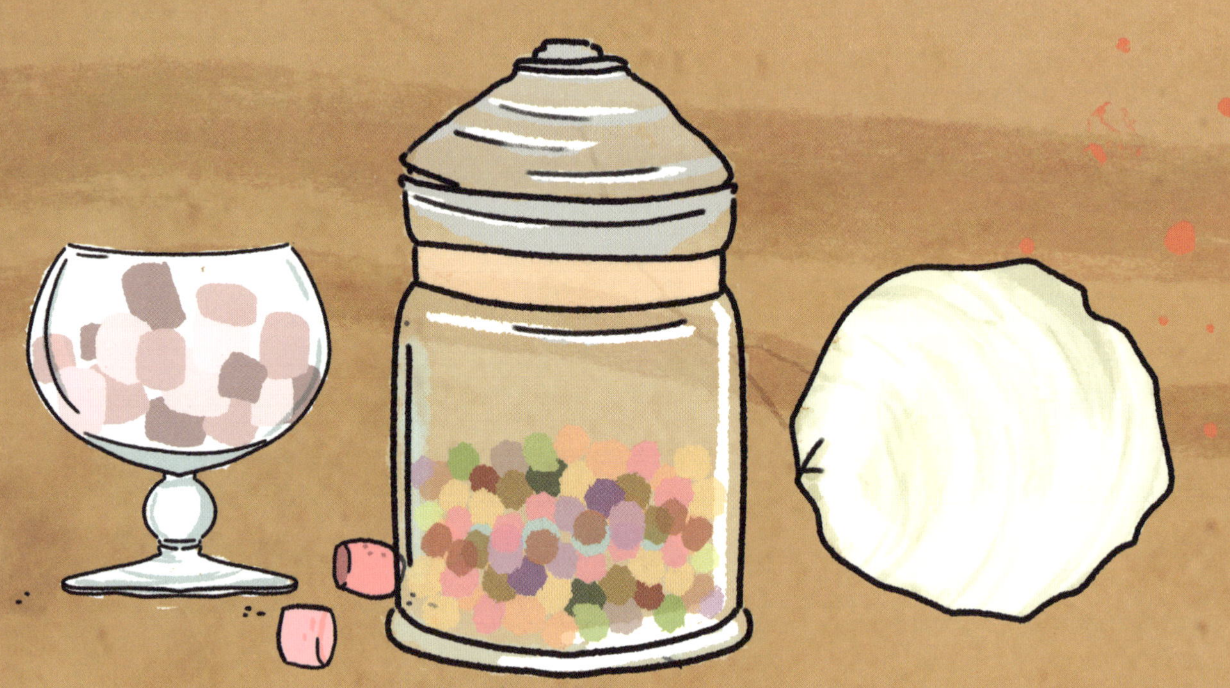

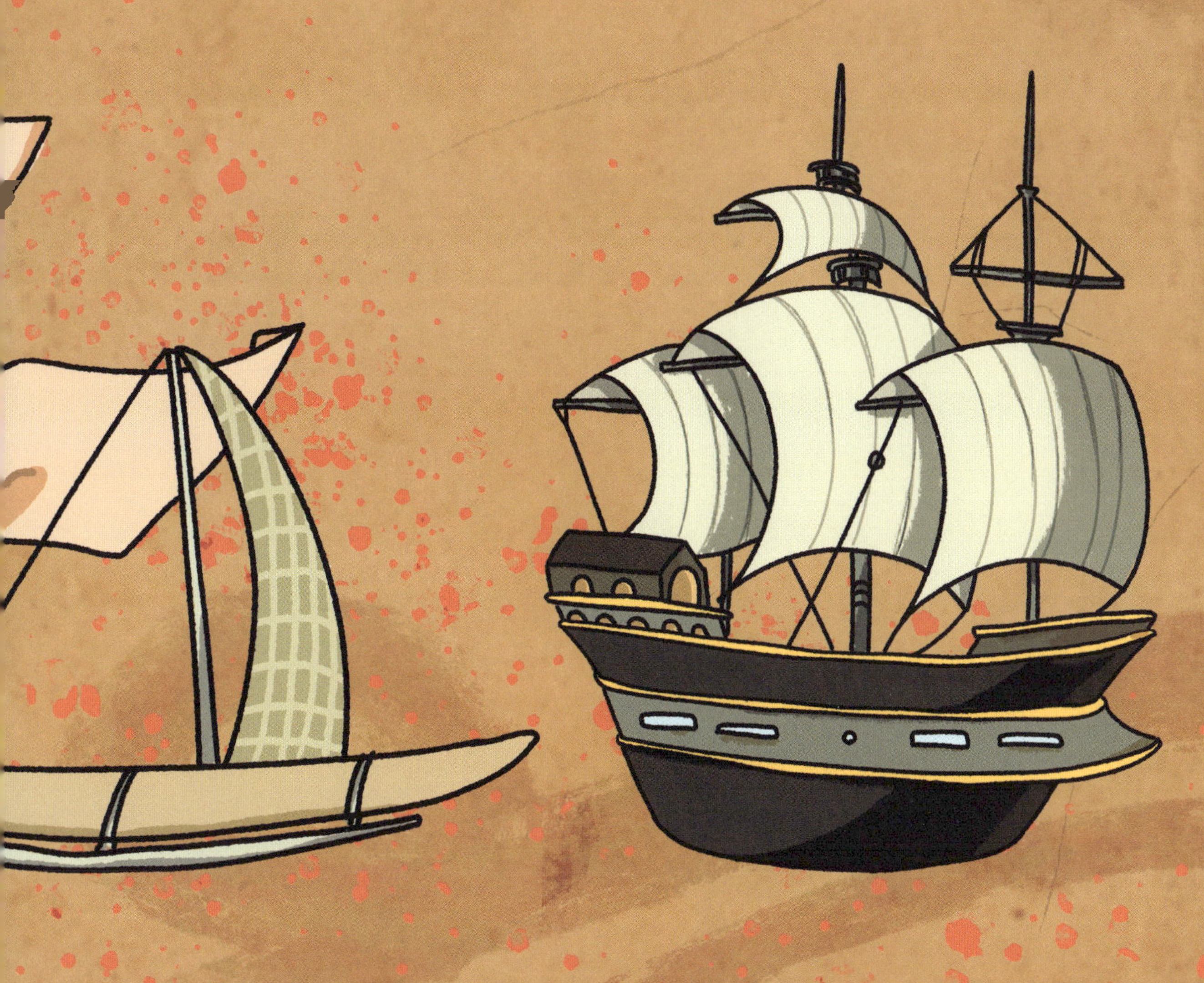

THE BOXER CODEX

The Boxer Codex was written around 1590. It is now owned by the Lilly Library at Indiana University in the USA and you can read it online. It not only contains images of the indigenous people of the Philippines but also those of other countries. See if you can find the indigenous people of your country in the Boxer Codex.

UNDERSTANDING YOUR ANCESTORS

Who are your ancestors? Do some of your own research on them by looking for old photographs or newspaper clippings from the past. This can help you learn what they looked like and how they lived. Stick your findings on these pages!

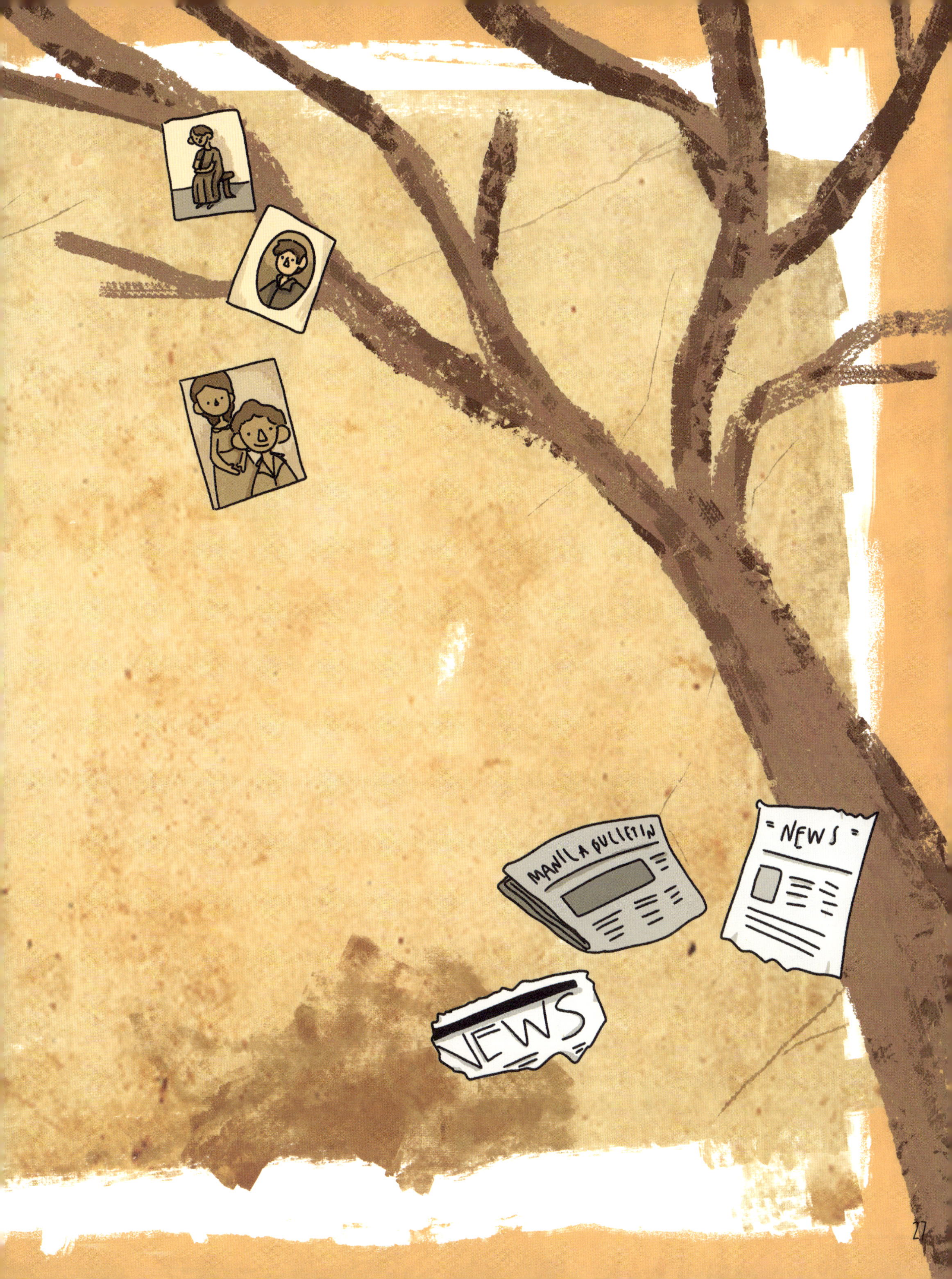
MANILA BULLETIN
NEWS
NEWS

DULANG BAYAN (A NATION'S DRAMA) (1982)

BY RENATO HABULAN

"Dulang bayan" means "a nation's drama" and that's just what artist Renato Habulan portrays in this dramatic three-part tableau. The upper part of the painting shows a group of people carrying a dead man wrapped in white cloth. Though they are in mourning, they stand with dignity and honour. The middle portion shows labourers and peasants at work under harsh conditions. Do you notice the heavy sack one of them carries, and the hats they wear? This implies they are labouring under the hot sun. In the lowest section, a group of people link their arms in anger and protest. United against exploitation and oppression, they are at their "tipping point." What do you think has upset them?

The painting reflects Mr Habulan's life experiences. He grew up in a poor community without water or electricity. They had to go to a fire hydrant two kilometres away to get drinking water. But Mr Habulan was less bothered by the poverty than the fear caused by corrupt politicians using money, guns and goons to rule. He remembers seeing several houses being destroyed because the owners did not vote for the "right" party.

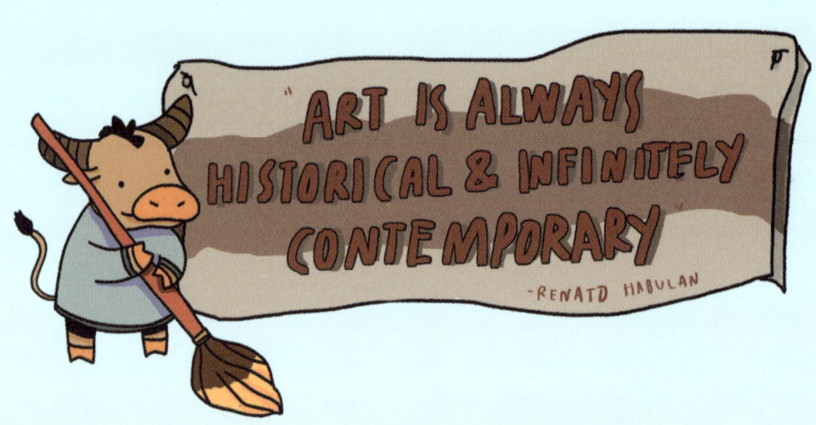

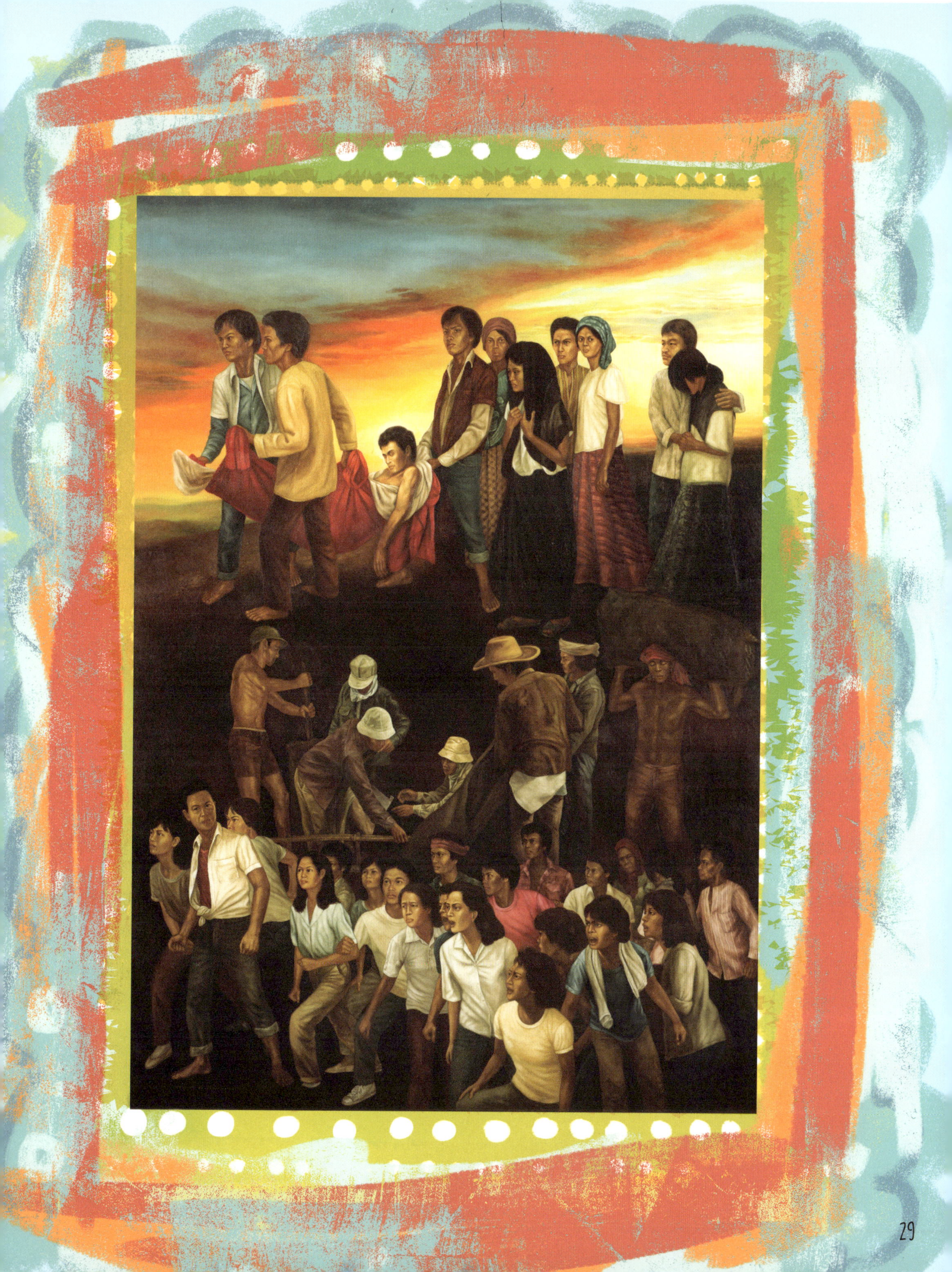

CARRYING IT FORWARD

Mr Habulan grew up with little money. While still in high school, he took vocational courses at night and apprenticed with an artist. Mr Habulan was creating paintings on canvas, which he later sold to pay for his tuition whilst in college at the University of the East School of Music and Fine Arts. Later, Mr Habulan's fellow artist Mr Gus Albor introduced him to an art patron who helped him pay for his college degree.

DID YOU KNOW?
A TABLEAU IS A DRAMATIC PORTRAYAL OF A SCENE OR A GROUP OF PEOPLE. OFTEN THE SCENE IS HIGHLY EMOTIONAL OR INVOLVES A SIGNIFICANT EVENT. WHAT OTHER SUBJECTS DO YOU THINK CAN BE PAINTED IN A TABLEAU?

Although he might have had the chance to study in Italy, Mr Habulan chose instead to live with ethnic communities and poor farmers. He realised that art could express the way these people felt, as *Dulang Bayan* (1982) does. As part of a theatre group, he painted murals that stood up for the people.

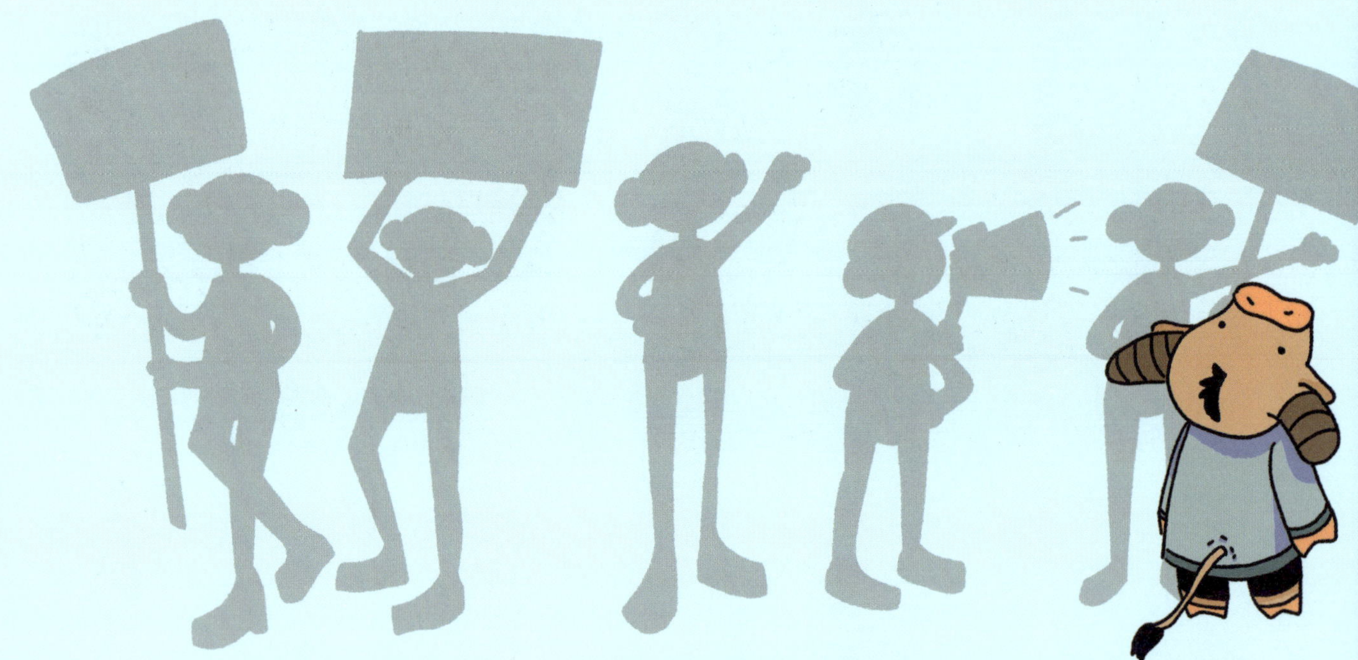

SPOT THE DIFFERENCE

Artists use colours to convey a mood or idea in a painting. In this painting, the dark colors emphasise the sadness and seriousness of the three scenes. Mr Habulan also uses a technique called *chiaroscuro* to give depth and create contrast between light and darkness. We learnt about *chiaroscuro* on page 10 with Mr de la Rosa's *Portrait of Jose Rizal* (1902). Does Mr Habulan use this technique differently from Mr de la Rosa? How?

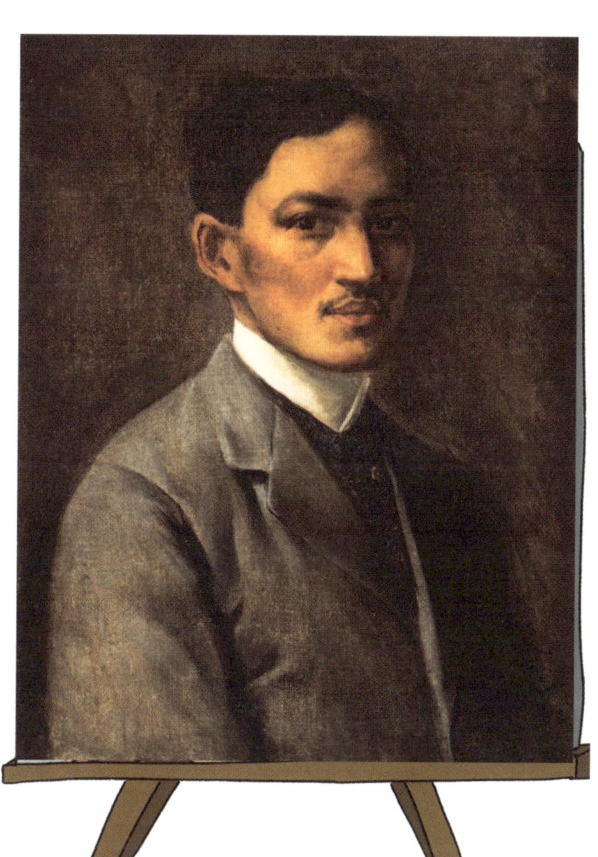

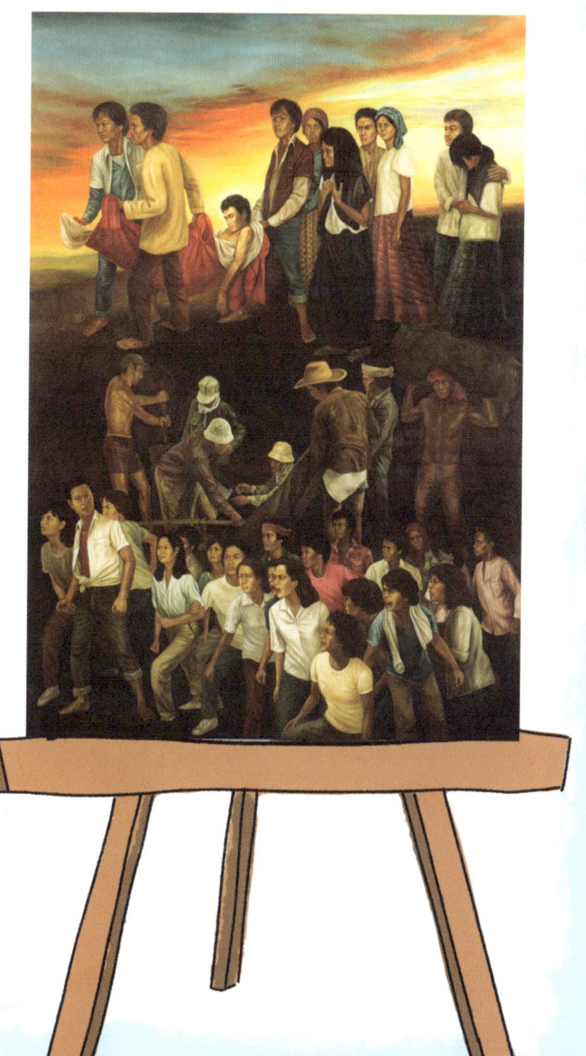

PARAISADO SORBETERO (ORANGE) (2004)

BY JOSE TENCE RUIZ

Wheeled carts, called *kariton*, are commonly seen on the crowded streets of Manila. They contain everything from clothes and shoes to fruits and vegetables. This orange cart looks like it could be selling ice cream. In fact, the work's title means "ice cream seller's paradise." Mr Ruiz coined the word "*paraisado*" from the Tagalog phrase "*paralisado ng paraiso*" meaning "paralyzed by paradise." Does he mean you can have too much of a good thing?

Instead of being filled with ice cream however, the structure atop this cart looks like a cathedral. On the upper right side is a tower, likely the belfry that houses the church bell. You can also see Gothic style arched windows all around the structure. What could Mr Ruiz mean by merging the features of religious architecture into a mobile *kariton*?

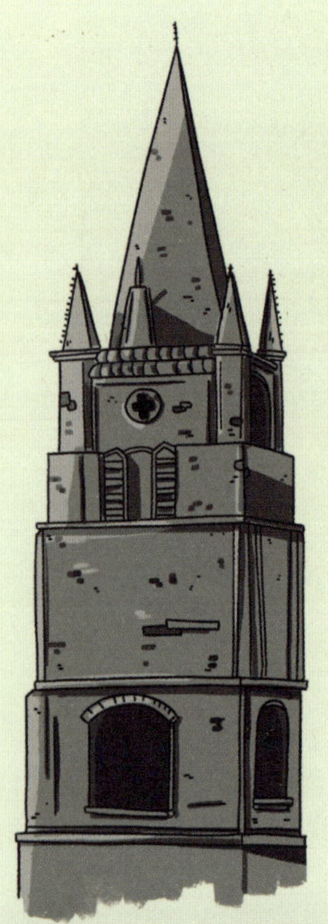

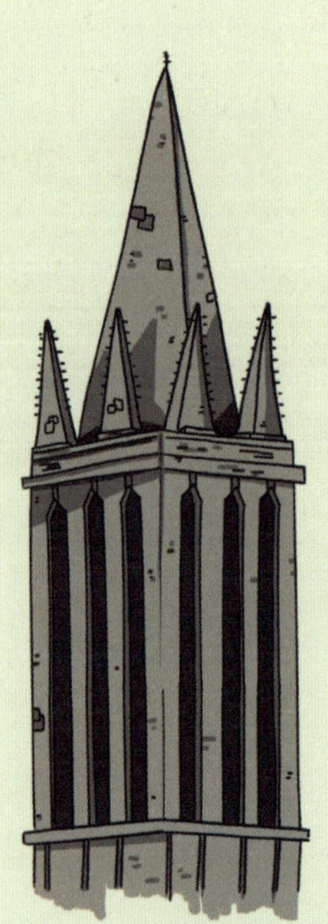

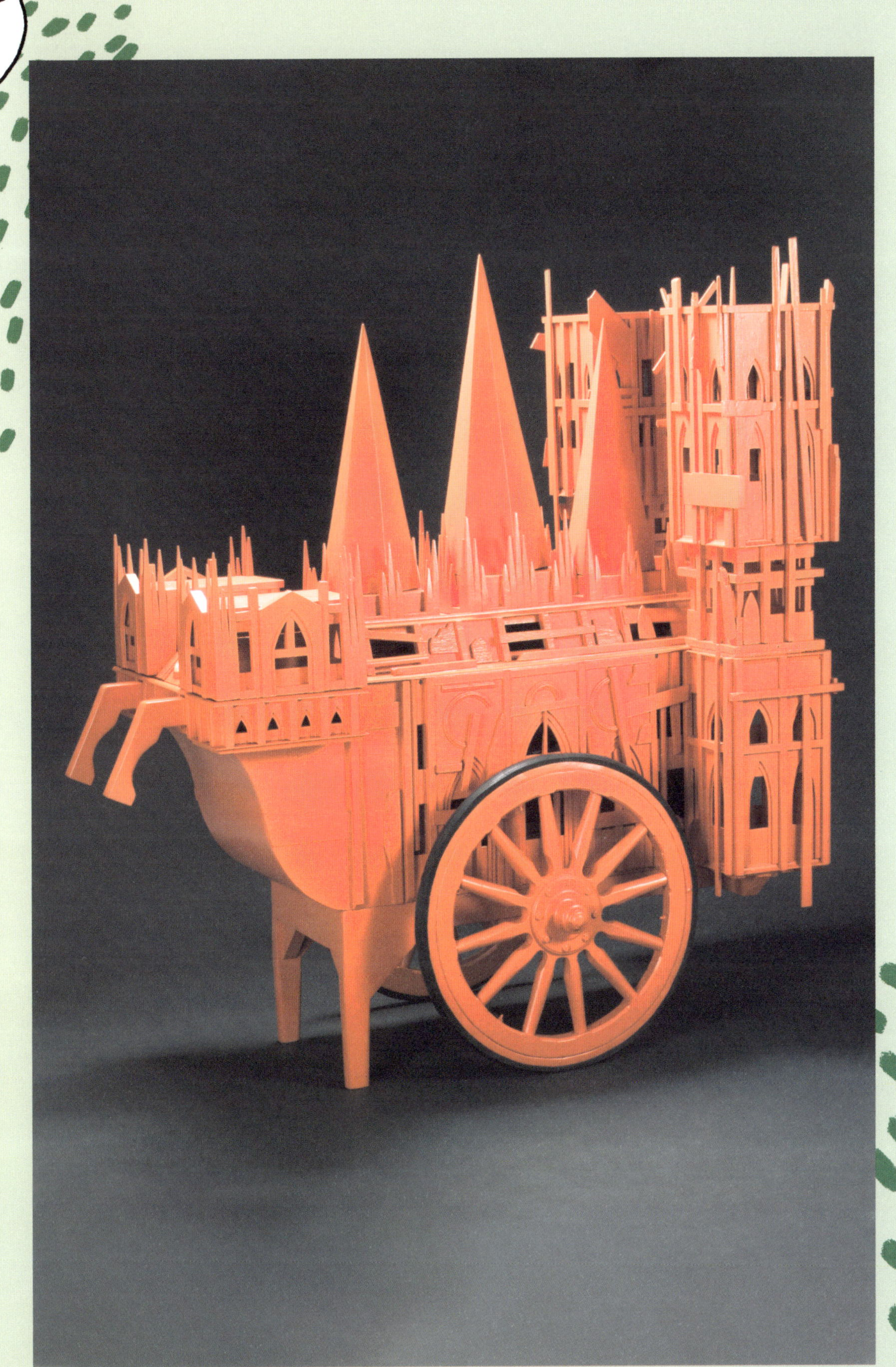

Mr Ruiz seems to be conveying the idea that religion (symbolised by the cathedral) is being peddled to the people, like cheap ice cream sold from a *kariton*. Although he grew up Catholic, Mr Ruiz was inspired to make this work because of his unhappiness with the Catholic Church. While he still believes in some ideas from Christianity, Mr Ruiz considers himself an agnostic, which means he believes that there may or may not be a god.

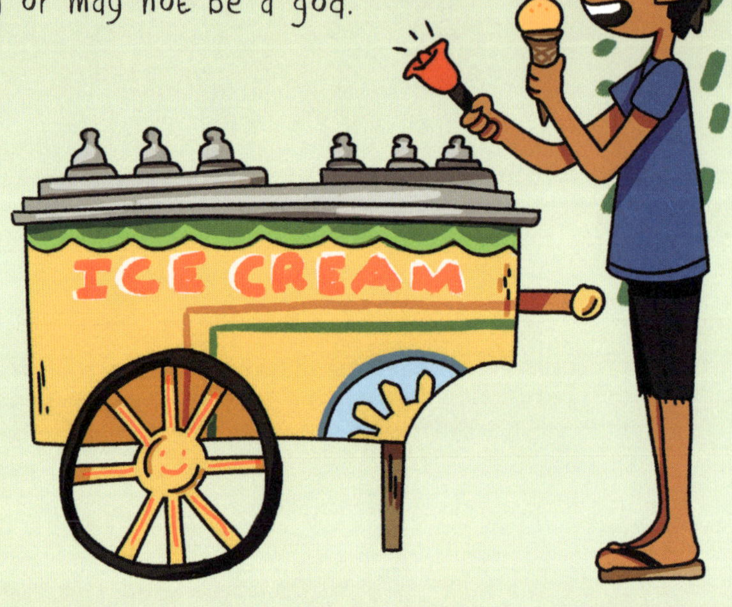

CREATING KARITON KATEDRALS

Born in the Philippines in 1956, Jose Tence Ruiz was a political cartoonist early in his career and continued as such in Singapore. It was while he was living in Singapore that he sketched the first *Sorbetero*. But it was only 10 years later, with the help of carpenter Mr Danilo Ilag-Ilag, that he was able to build it. So far, he has built 14 *Kariton Katedrals*. Each takes nine months to complete!

FILL UP YOUR OWN KARITON!

What else could you construct on a *kariton*? Fill in your cart with a structure or building you think could be mobile!

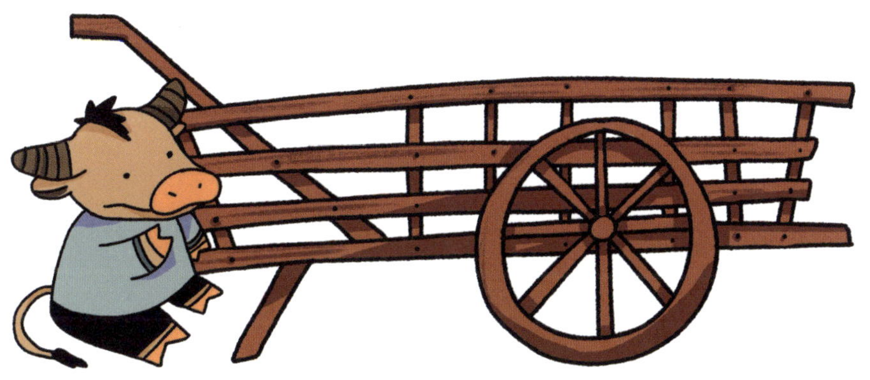

DANCING MUTANTS (1965)

BY HERNANDO R. OCAMPO

Look at this painting. What do you see? The elongated wisps of red, green and orange look like scorched leaves, but could they also be a cluster of flickering flames? Now, try looking at the painting from afar. You might perhaps detect an outstretched arm, a blank face or a group of humans clinging to each other. Could they be figures swaying in the wind?

This painting was inspired by Hernando R. Ocampo's imagination of what could happen in a nuclear war. Would humans become unusual-looking mutants instead? Mr Ocampo tried to explore this question during what he called his Mutants Period, from 1963 to 1968.

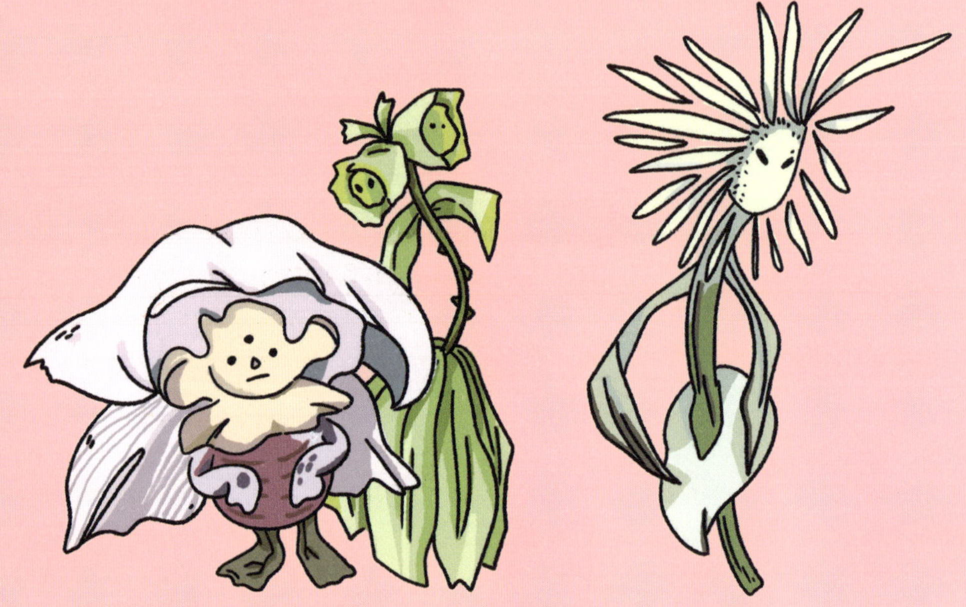

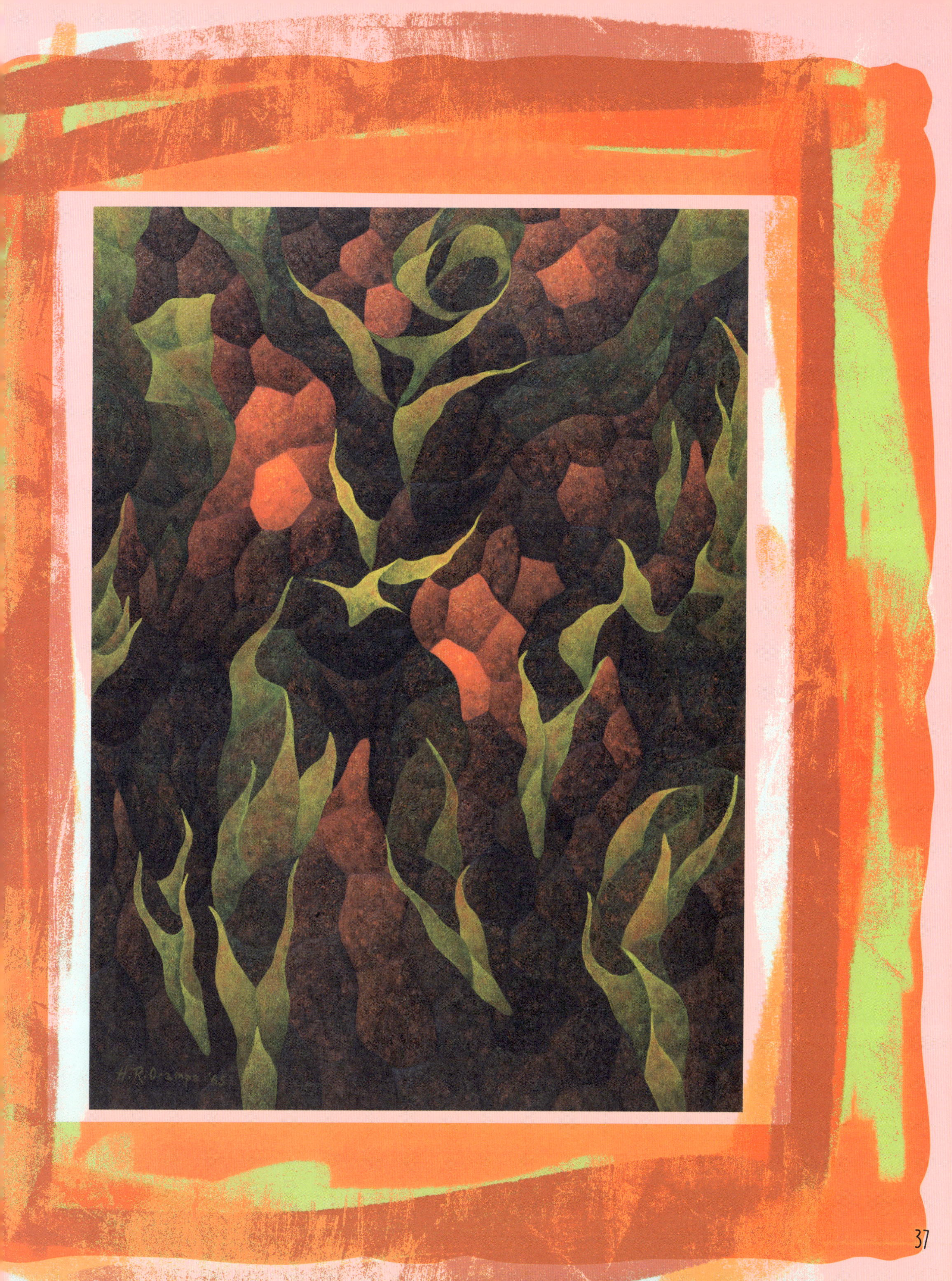

Mr Ocampo described his later paintings as "visual melodies," and there is melody in this painting too! The colours he used are not in their pure form but tinged with other hues. The red could be tinted with white, yellow or even some black and green. How do these different colours make the painting feel? They may hint at darker possibilities, like the frightening prospect of human mutation!

Mr Ocampo never once travelled overseas because a fortune teller told him he would die in an airplane. Hence, he is said to be a homegrown Filipino artist. His works were mostly influenced by his surroundings: the colour of sunshine, the sound of the pouring rain, the beauty of the flowers, and of the birds, shells and sea creatures of his country, as well as by television films and movies.

ABOUT HERNANDO R. OCAMPO

Hernando R. Ocampo studied law, commerce and creative writing. He never received formal artistic training, but became one of the Philippines' most important artists. He was a leading member of the Neo-Realists, a group of artists who emerged after World War II. Mr Ocampo has won numerous awards from the Art Association of the Philippines. In 1991, 13 years after his death, he was posthumously named National Artist in Visual Arts by the Philippine government.

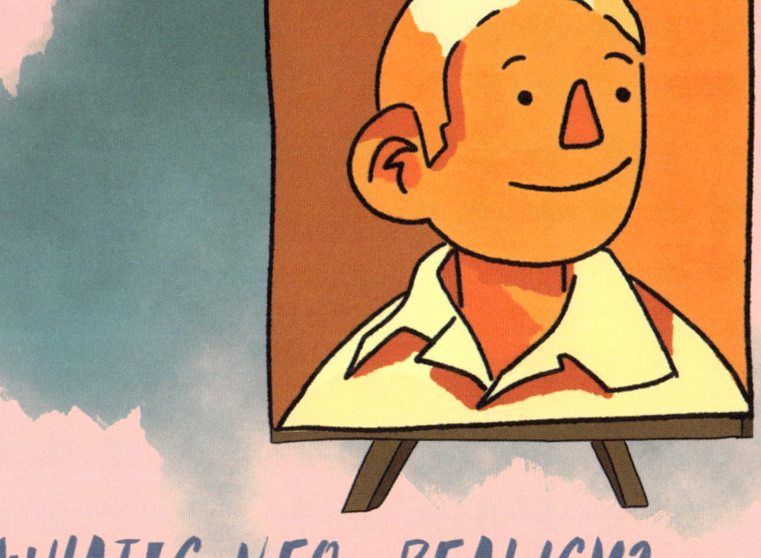

WHAT'S NEO-REALISM?

Before Neo-Realism came about in the Philippines, artists concentrated on capturing the imagined beauty in their surroundings. However, reality was anything but. The country was ravaged by war and poverty. Neo-Realists put these horrors into painting by depicting the inner reality of these experiences. They used line, colour, form, texture and composition to do so.

PAINT LIKE HERNANDO R. OCAMPO!

Below is an image of Mr Ocampo. Do you see what's on the canvas behind him? He has numbered each different section and filled in the sections with different colours. This is known as painting by numbers.

Mr Ocampo created a similar activity for the *Philippine Panorama* magazine. Colour your own Ocampo on the opposite page!

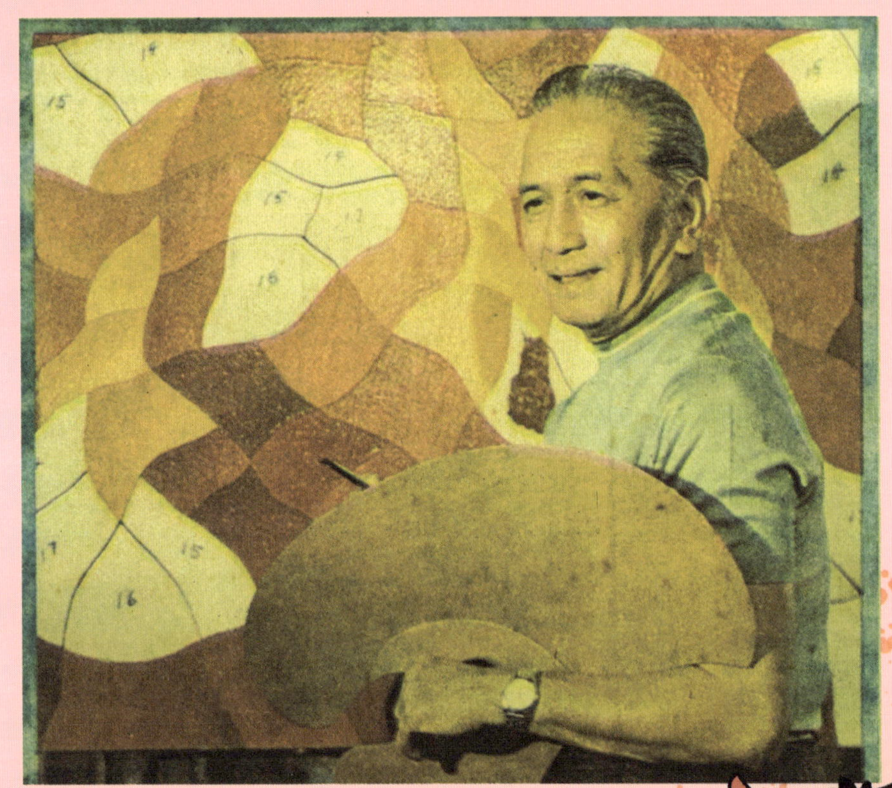

Hernando R. Ocampo painting by numbers
Image from the *Manila Chronicle*, 30 April 1972

COLOR YOUR OWN OCAMPO

COLORING INSTRUCTIONS

1 CADMIUM YELLOW LIGHT
2 CADMIUM ORANGE
3 CADMIUM ORANGE
4 CADMIUM ORANGE
5 CADMIUM RED LIGHT
6 CADMIUM RED LIGHT
7 CADMIUM RED LIGHT
8 CADMIUM VERMILLON
9 CADMIUM VERMILLON
10 CADMIUM VERMILLON
11 GRUMBACHER REI
12 GRUMBACHER REI
13. GRUMBACHER REI
14. IVORY BLACK
15. IVORY BLACK
16 IVORY BLACK
17 IVORY BLACK
18 Use your imaginatio
in your own color

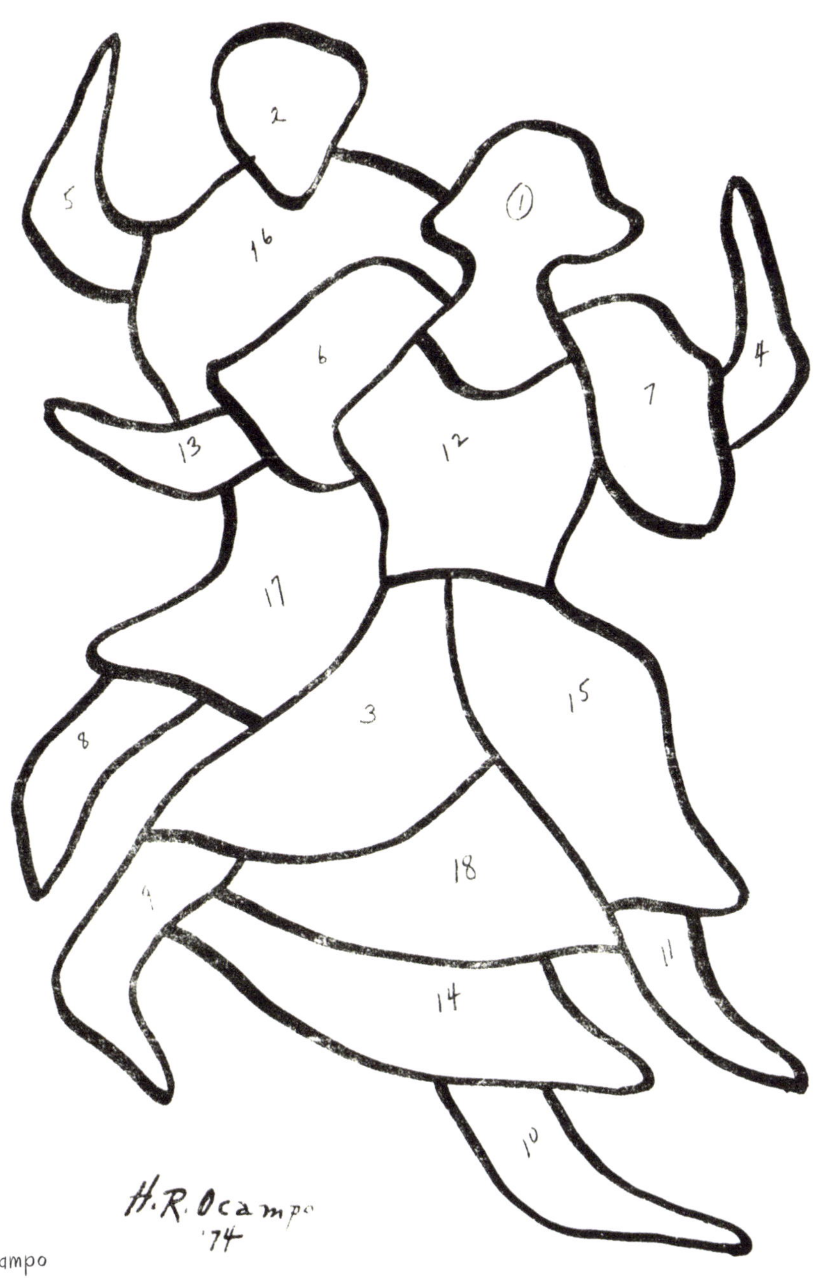

Color Your Own Ocampo
Hernando R. Ocampo
1974
Image permission courtesy of *Manila Bulletin*

EVIL EYE (1983)

BY PACITA ABAD

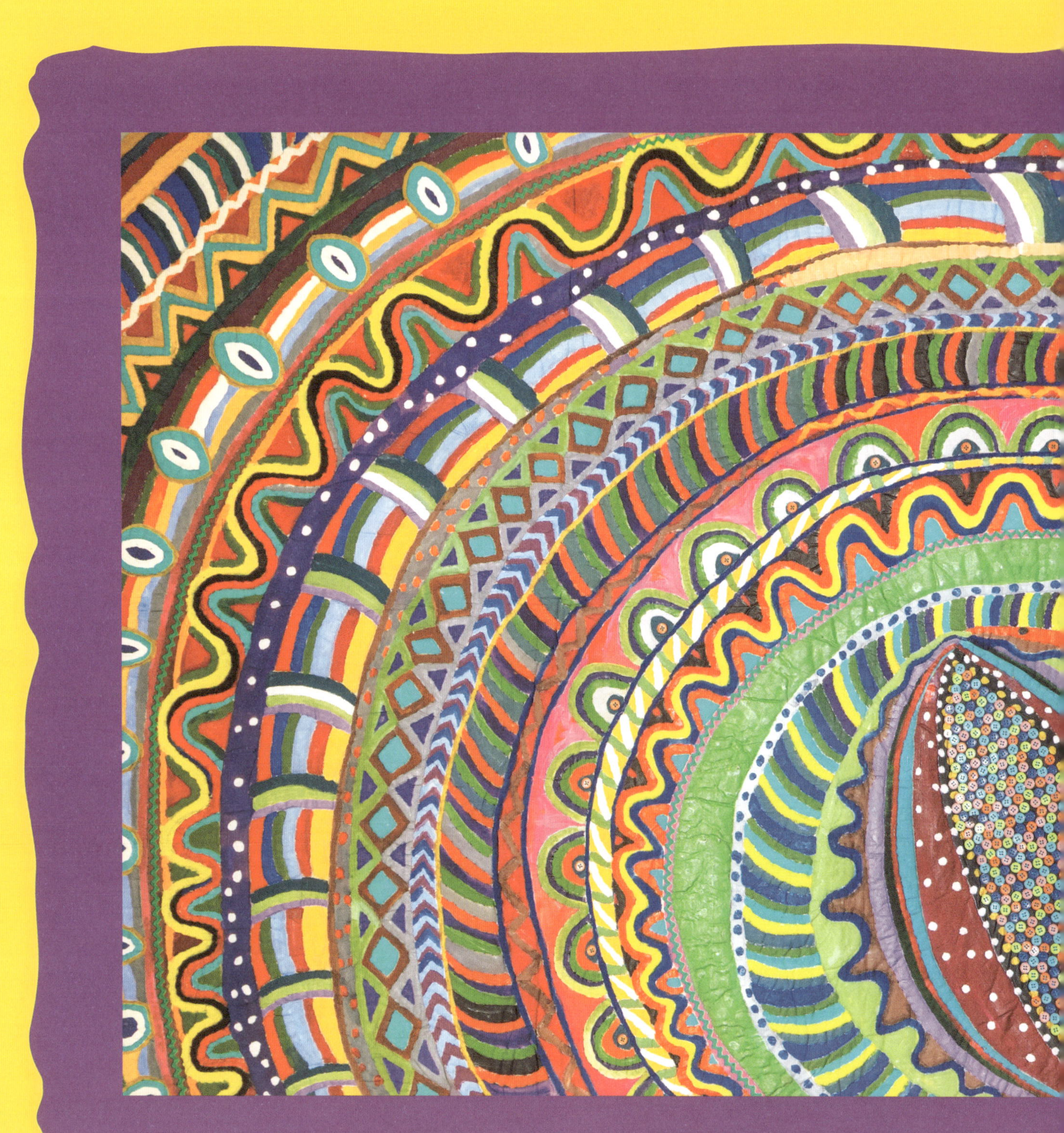

This work is based on the ancient belief of the evil eye. From the beginning of civilisation, people have believed that the evil eye is a curse, that anyone given the evil eye would have bad luck. The artist Pacita Abad took this belief and created a piece of art based on it.

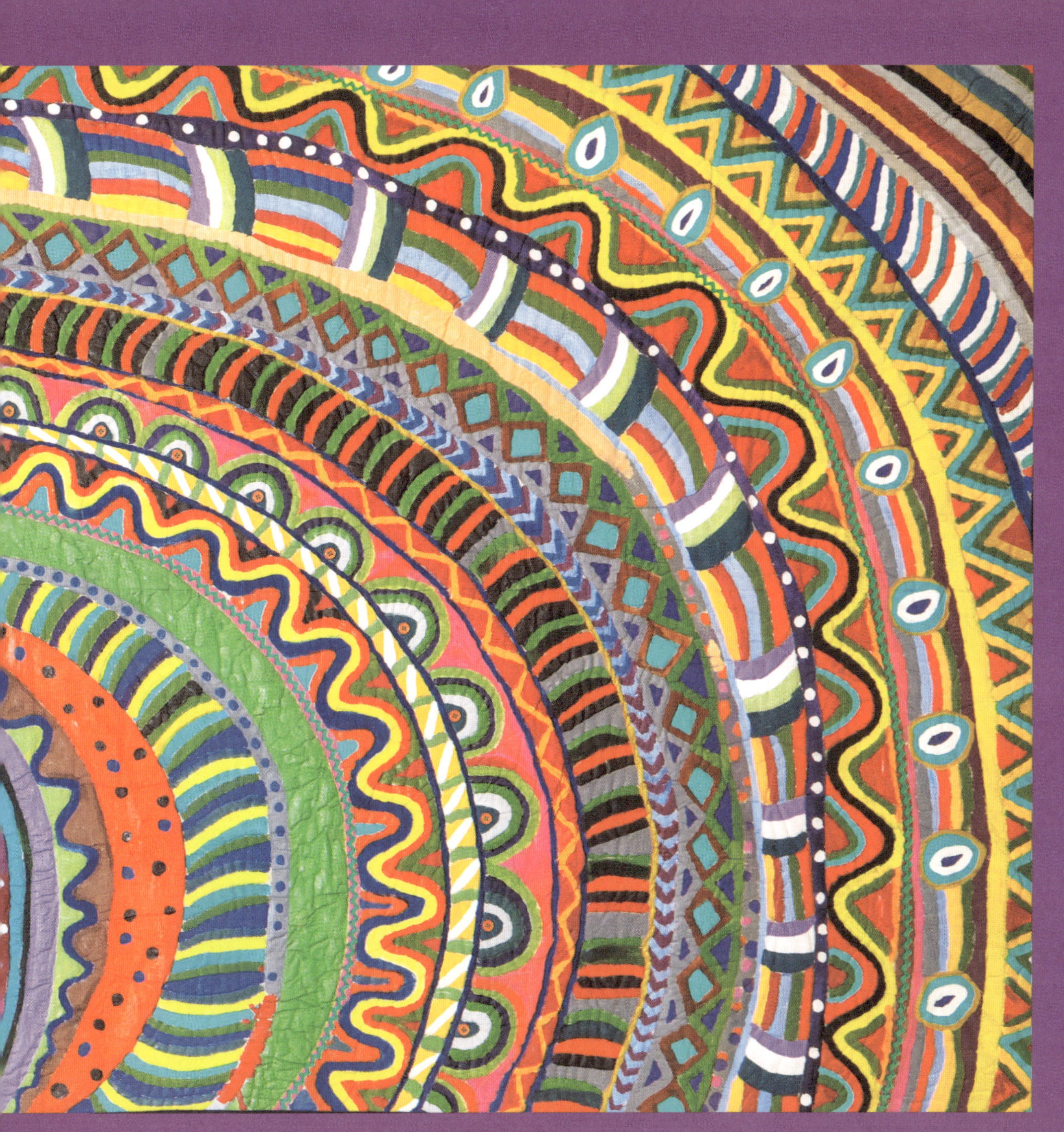

Ms Abad used plastic buttons, thread, rickrack, fabric and acrylic paint to create this beautiful tapestry. She stitched these elements in circular arcs growing concentrically from small to big. Although the various elements are arranged in neat, symmetrical order, Ms Abad made the work more dynamic by using different patterns, from dots to waves, triangles to ovals. Also, the repeated colours like red, green, yellow and blue unite these patterns and make the work look coherent.

DID YOU KNOW?
ANCIENT CULTURES BELIEVED THAT THERE ARE WAYS TO PROTECT YOURSELF FROM THE EVIL EYE. AMULETS, CHARMS AND SOME PRECIOUS STONES ARE SAID TO COUNTER THE EFFECTS OF THE EVIL EYE.

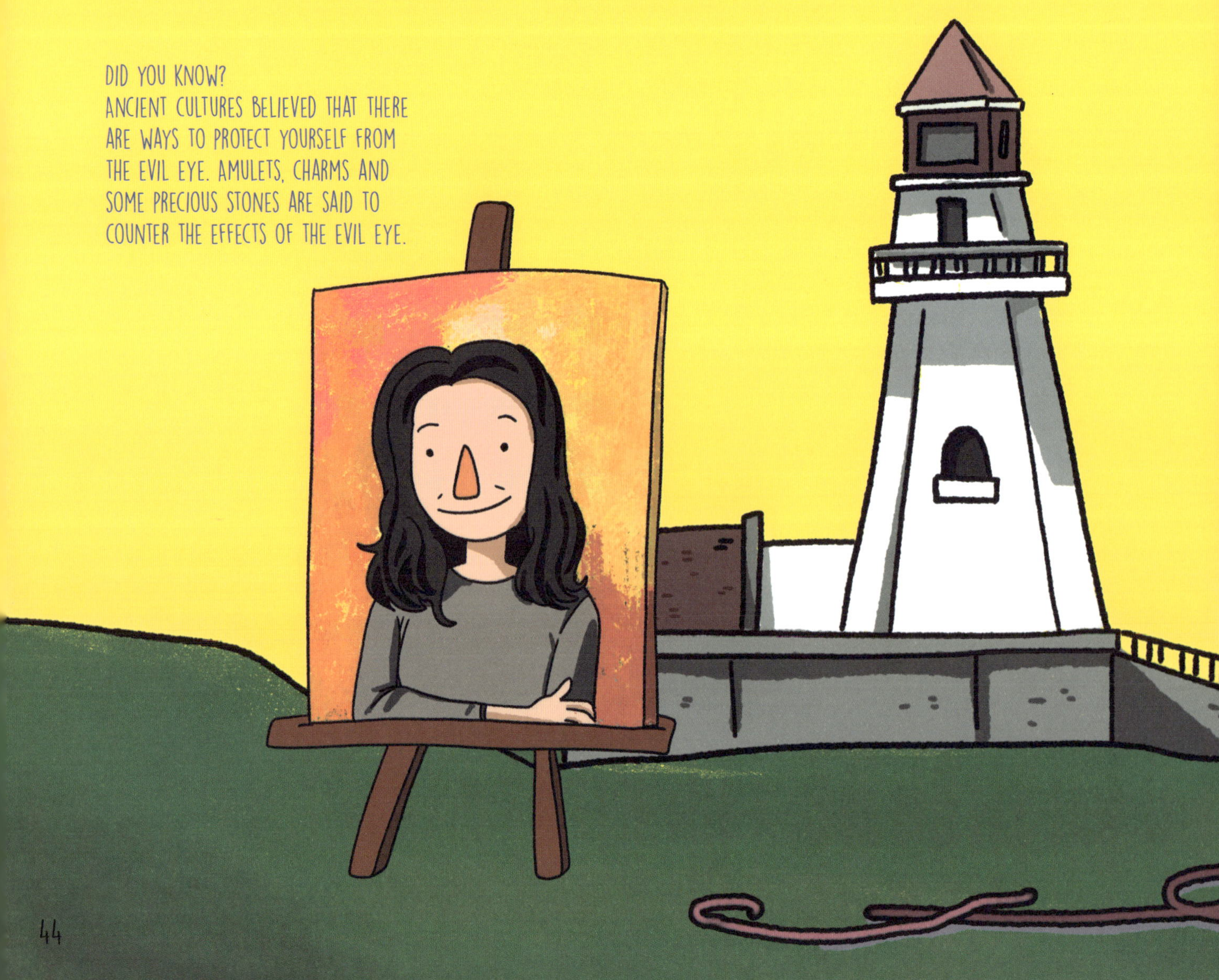

AROUND THE WORLD WITH PACITA ABAD

Pacita Abad was born in Basco, Batanes, a windswept island in the northernmost part of the Philippines. After finishing college at the University of the Philippines, she left for Madrid where she planned to study law. But while on a stopover in San Francisco, she changed her mind. She decided to stay in the United States instead, and ended up studying art in Washington DC and New York.

After she became an artist, Ms Abad travelled far and wide. She traversed all the continents (except Antarctica!) and visited over 80 countries, some of which she lived in for extended periods of time. Wherever she was, she would pick up ideas and inspiration for her art.

Ms Abad created over 3,500 art works in her lifetime, and held over 60 solo exhibitions at museums and galleries around the world. Bright, vibrant colours and exuberance characterise Ms Abad's works, whether they are paintings, installations or *trapunto*.

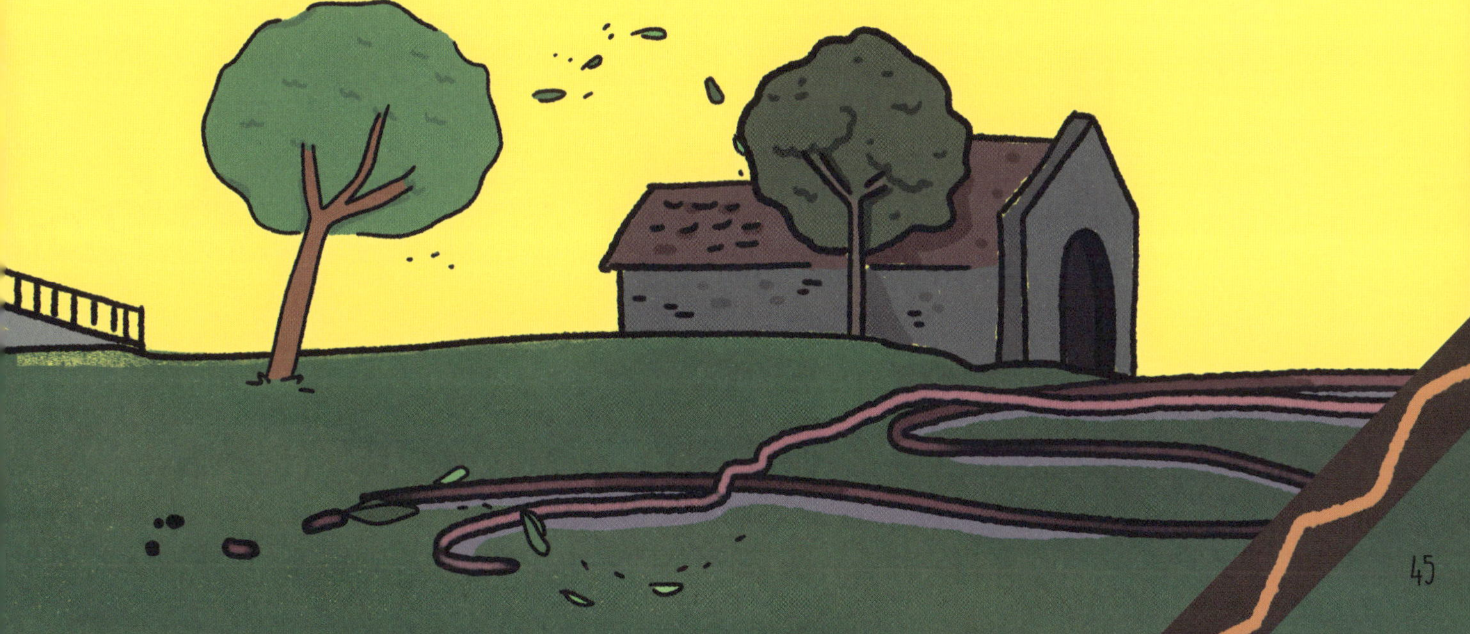

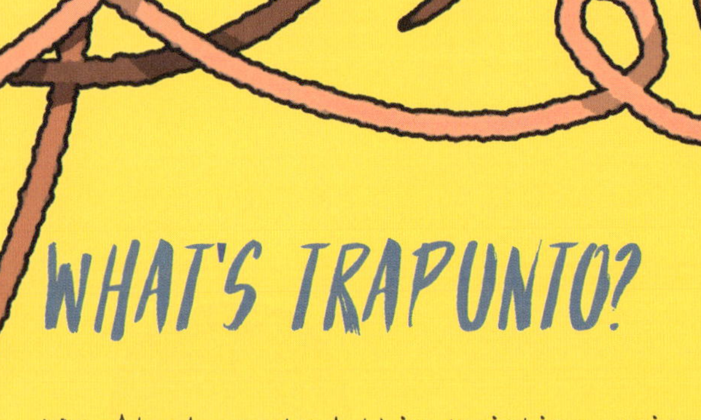

WHAT'S TRAPUNTO?

Ms Abad created this painting using a method called *trapunto*. Started in Sicily, Italy in the 14th century, *trapunto* is a quilting technique that creates a puffy surface. If you were to see *Evil Eye* (1983) in real life, you would see that its surface is not flat, but raised and textured. The fabric, buttons and acrylic also enrich the work with different textures.

How do you think this work would feel to the touch?

PRICKLY

ROUGH

SMOOTH

HARD

WRINKLY

LUMPY

SOFT

BUMPY

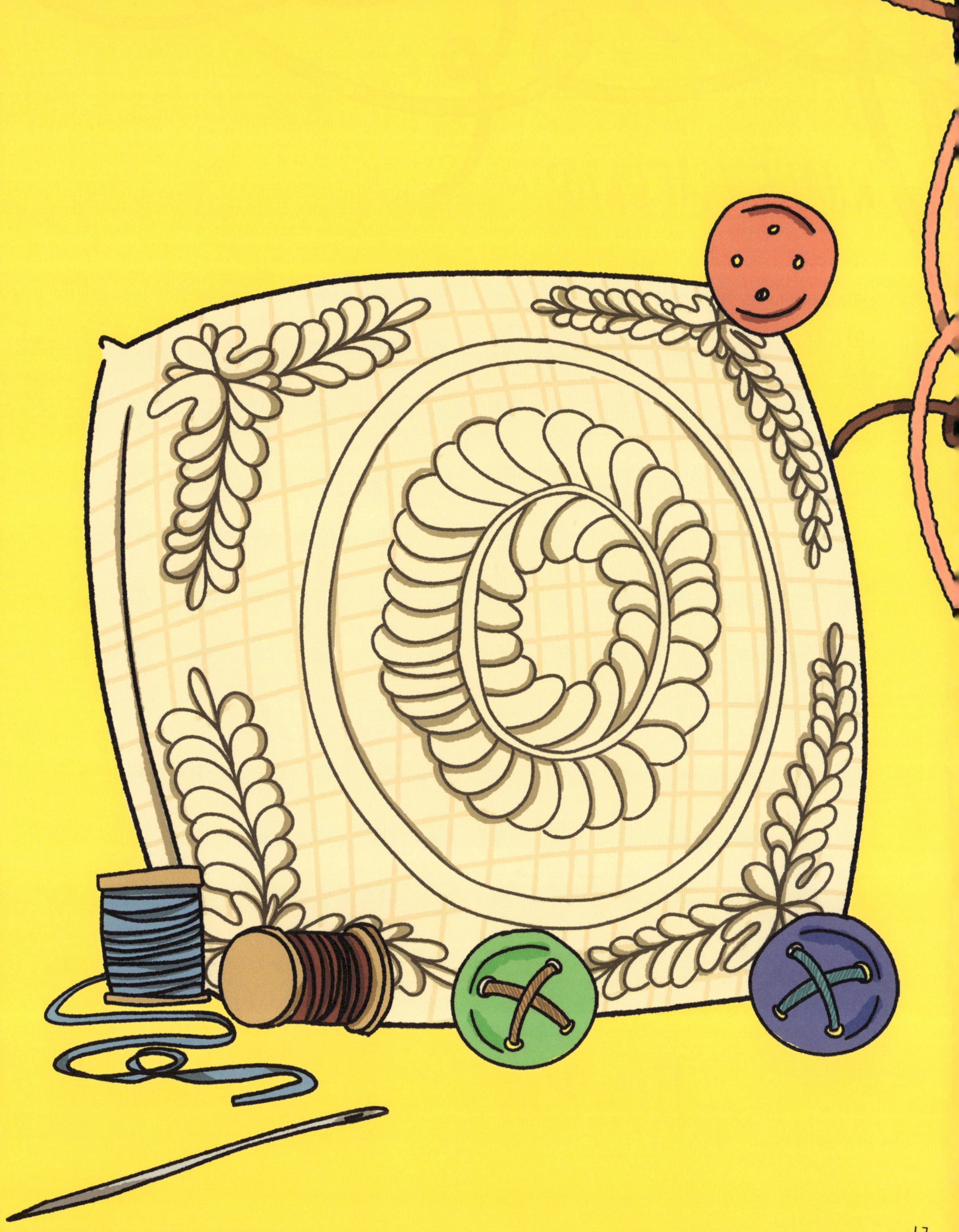

THE CREATION MYTHS (2009)
BY RODEL TAPAYA

Can a bird be larger than a pack of dogs? Can animals be created from feathers? They can, if they're in the painting *The Creation Myths* (2009) by artist Rodel Tapaya.

At the center of *The Creation Myths* (2009) is Manaul. This mythical bird has feathers that can transform into animals and human beings. Do you see this transformation already happening near the nest of eggs? Sitting above the nest is Kan-Laon. He is the Creator and the King of Time, watching his creations emerge from a distance.

With his three dogs on the left side of the canvas is Kabigat. He created the mountains with the rain god Baiyuhibi, whom you can also see in this painting.

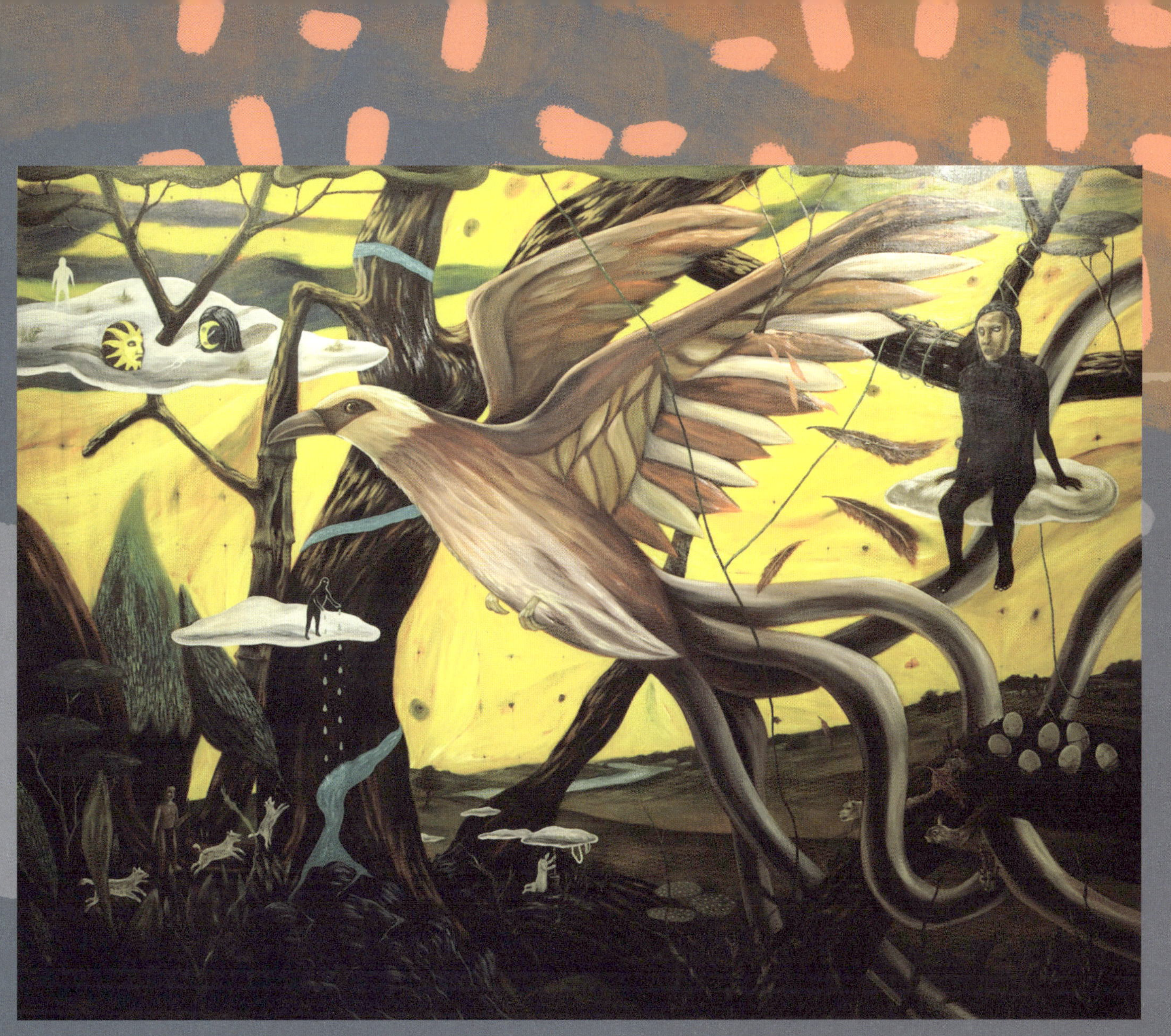

Can you spot the sun and moon on a cloud above? They are Apolaqui (the sun) and Mayari (the moon). You may also be able to spot two figures peeping out from a narrow crack below them. This depicts the legend of how the first man and woman were born: they emerged from a bamboo pole cracked open by a bird!

The many elements in this painting weave their own narratives from legends and folk tales that have been told across generations. Although no one really knows where these stories came from, Mr Tapaya uses his imagination to bring them to life. There are more stories to explore: What do you think will hatch from the eggs in the nest?

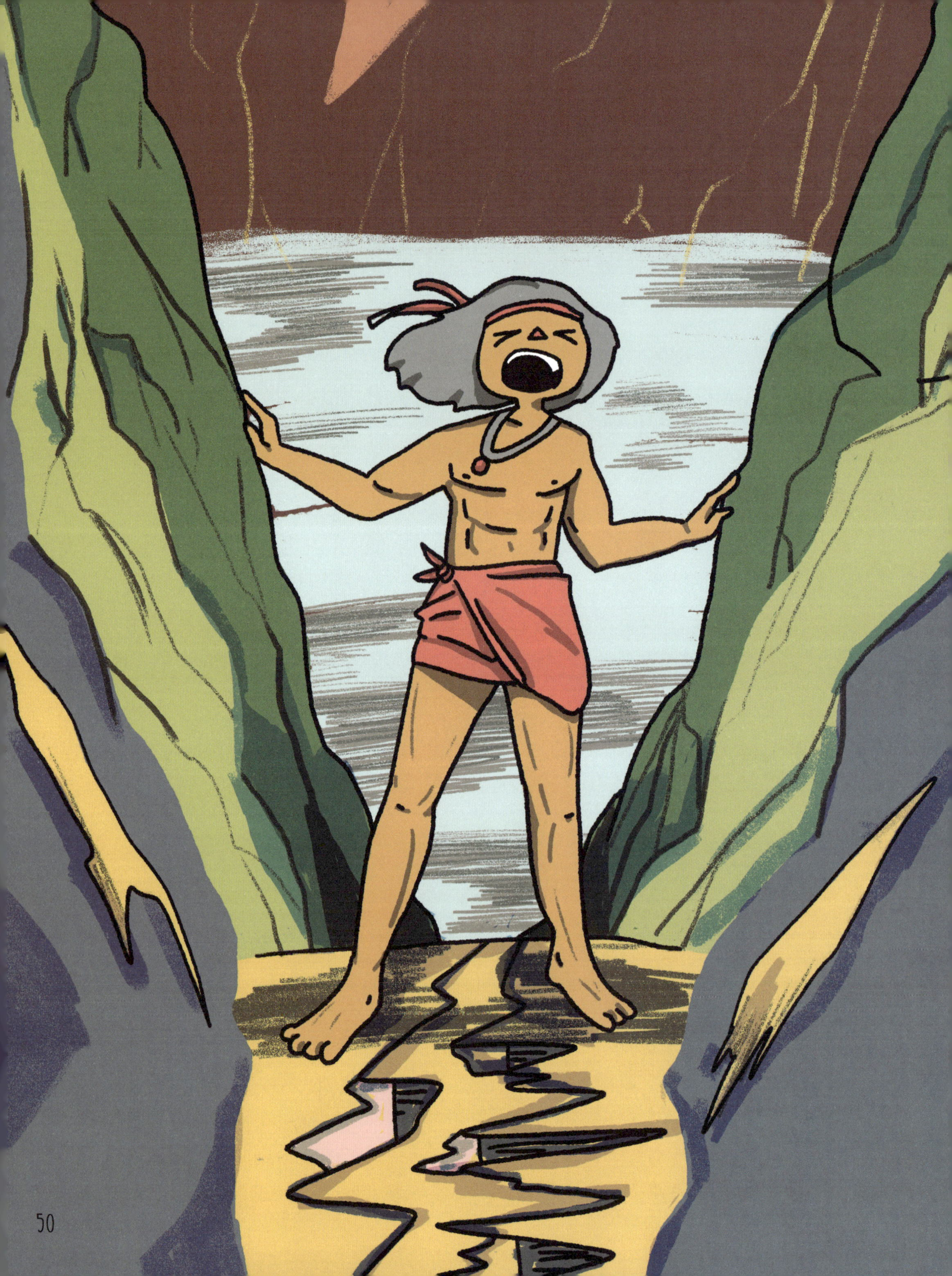

RODEL TAPAYA AND THE MOUNTAINS OF MONTALBAN

Rodel Tapaya was born in Montalban, Rizal, where the mountains were a big part of his childhood imagination. When he was seven years old, he heard the tale of Bernardo Carpio, a giant who tried to stop two mountains from fighting. According to legend, Bernardo Carpio got trapped between the mountains of Montalban. Convinced this was true, Mr Tapaya hiked to the mountains in search of the giant and the handprints people say he left behind.

Mr Tapaya's fascination with local myths and legends continued to adulthood. Stories of legends and mythical creatures fire his imagination and inspire his paintings. These myths and folk stories help him find his identity and sense of belonging. Like *The Creation Myths* (2009), his paintings are as immersive as the stories they tell.

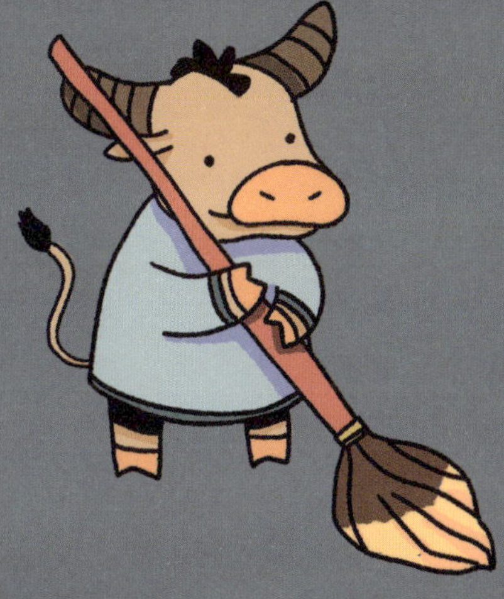

DRAW YOUR FOLKLORE

There are many mythical creatures in Philippine folklore, such as: The *tikbalang*, a half-human half-horse figure, the *kapre*, a giant who lives on top of tall trees and often smokes cigars, and the *sarimanok*, a colourful magical bird that symbolises good fortune.

Imagine what these creatures may look like, then make your own drawings of them on the blank page! Then look at the illustrations on the next page - are they the same as what you envisioned?

ARE THEY WHAT YOU IMAGINED?

Here are drawings of the *kapre*, *tikbalang* and *sarimanok* based on what many who hear those folklores imagine they look like.

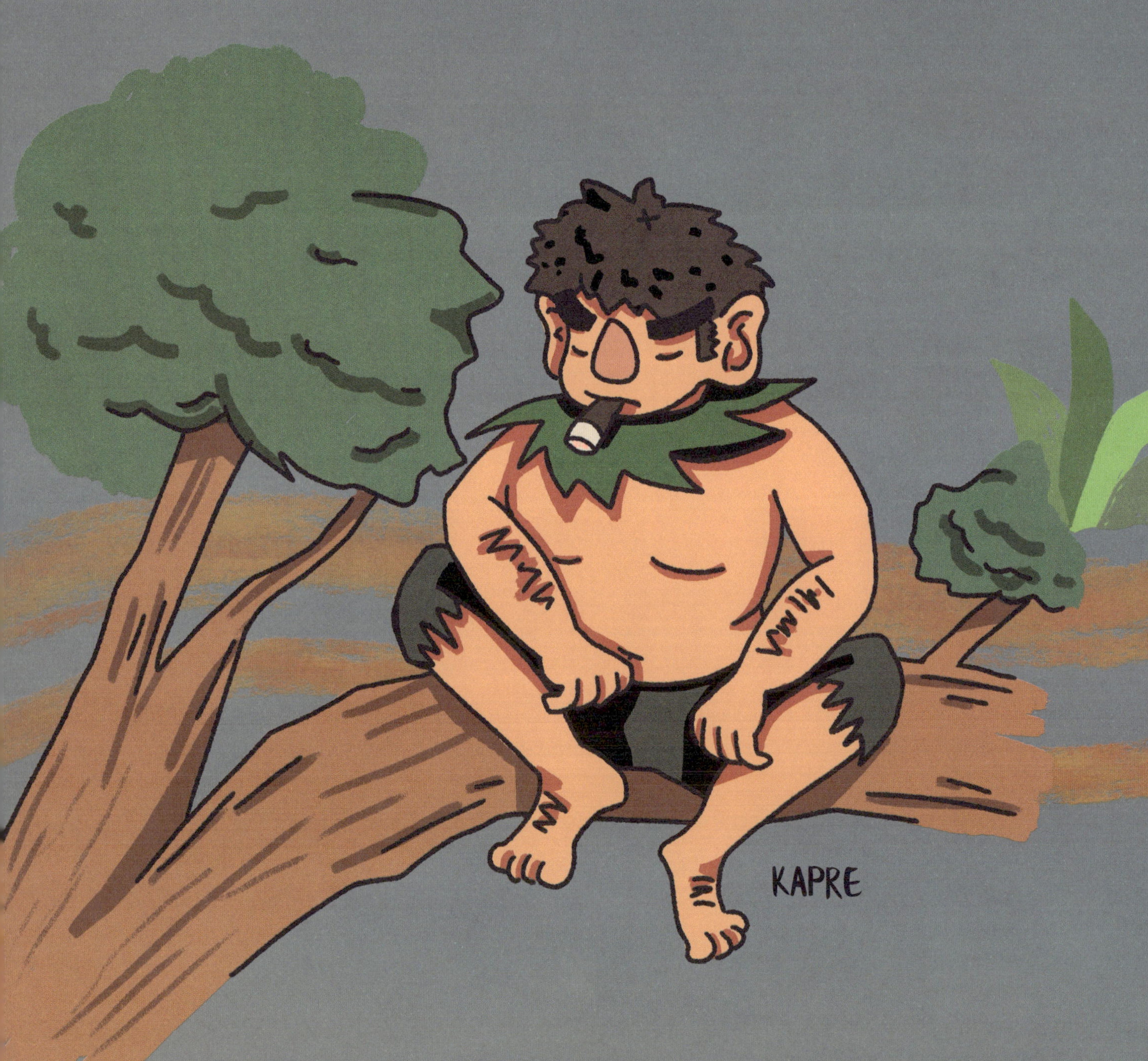

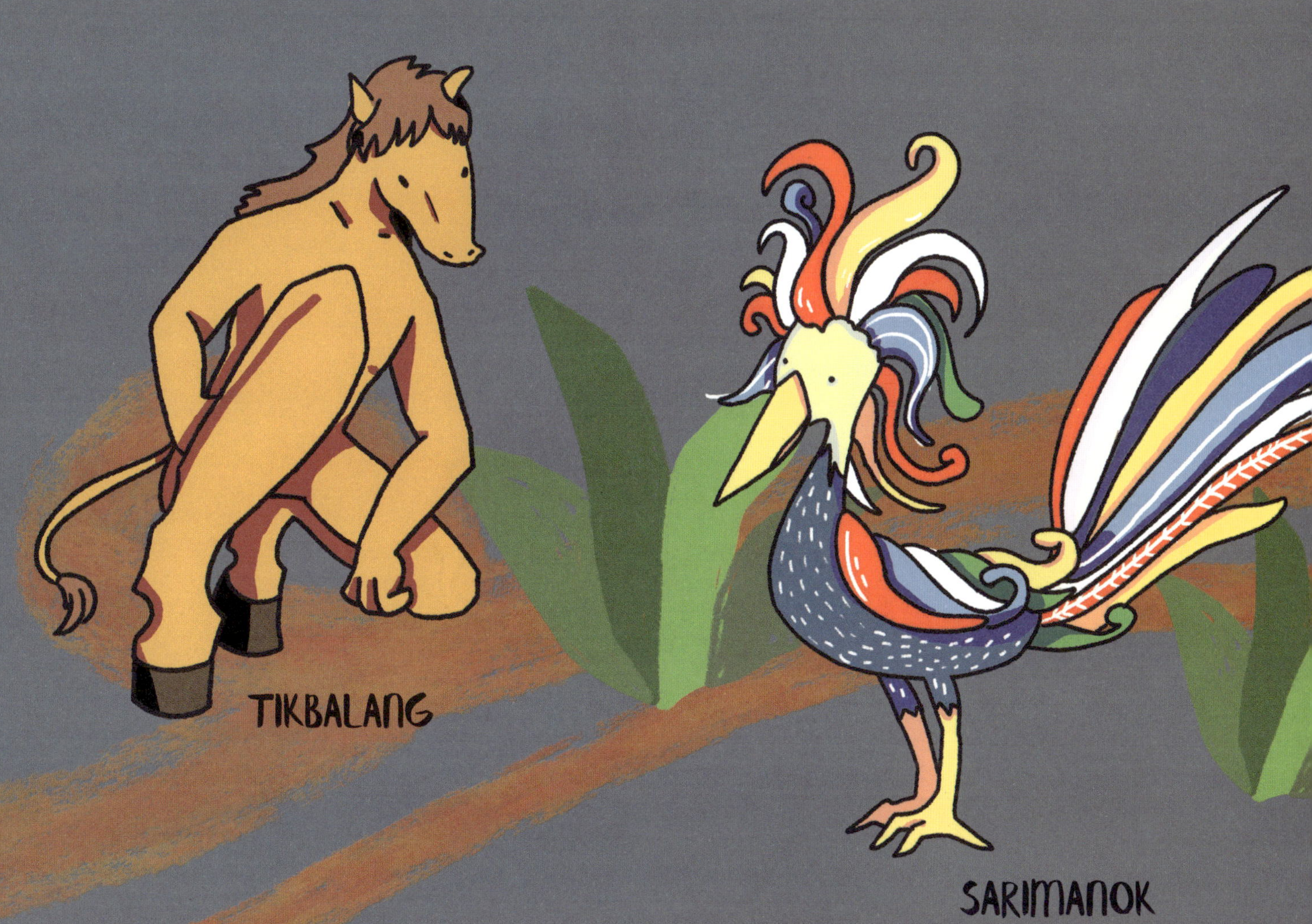
TIKBALANG
SARIMANOK

CLOUD CANYONS NO. 24 (2015, FIRST VERSION IN SERIES 1964)

BY DAVID MEDALLA

Playing with soap bubbles can be a lot of fun! Can it also be art?

In this work, artist David Medalla creates art with soap bubbles. He uses wood, plastic, compressors, a timer, water and detergent to create the illusion of a dramatic landscape formed from clouds. The mixture of water and detergent forms bubbles at the bottom, which then rise up the tubes. Once they reach the top, the bubbles emerge as soft clusters. The bubbles are continuously emerging, constantly creating new shapes. Do these clouds remind you of the frothy cream atop an ice cream soda? Or toothpaste squeezed out of the tube?

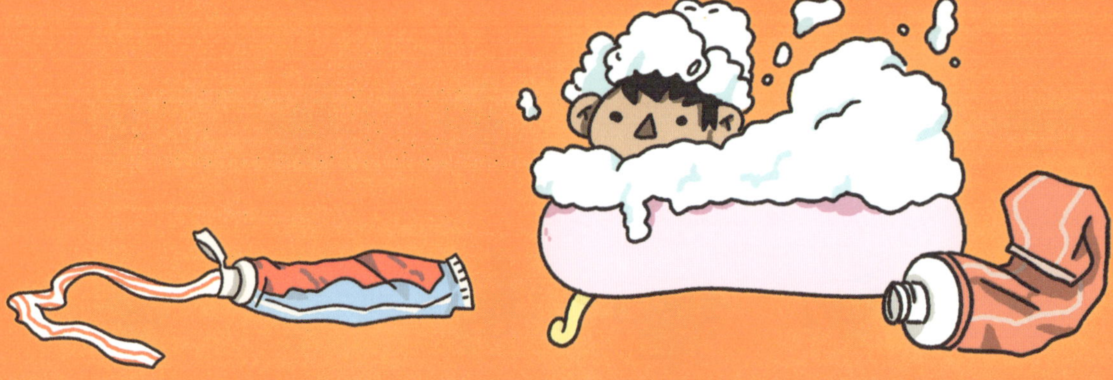

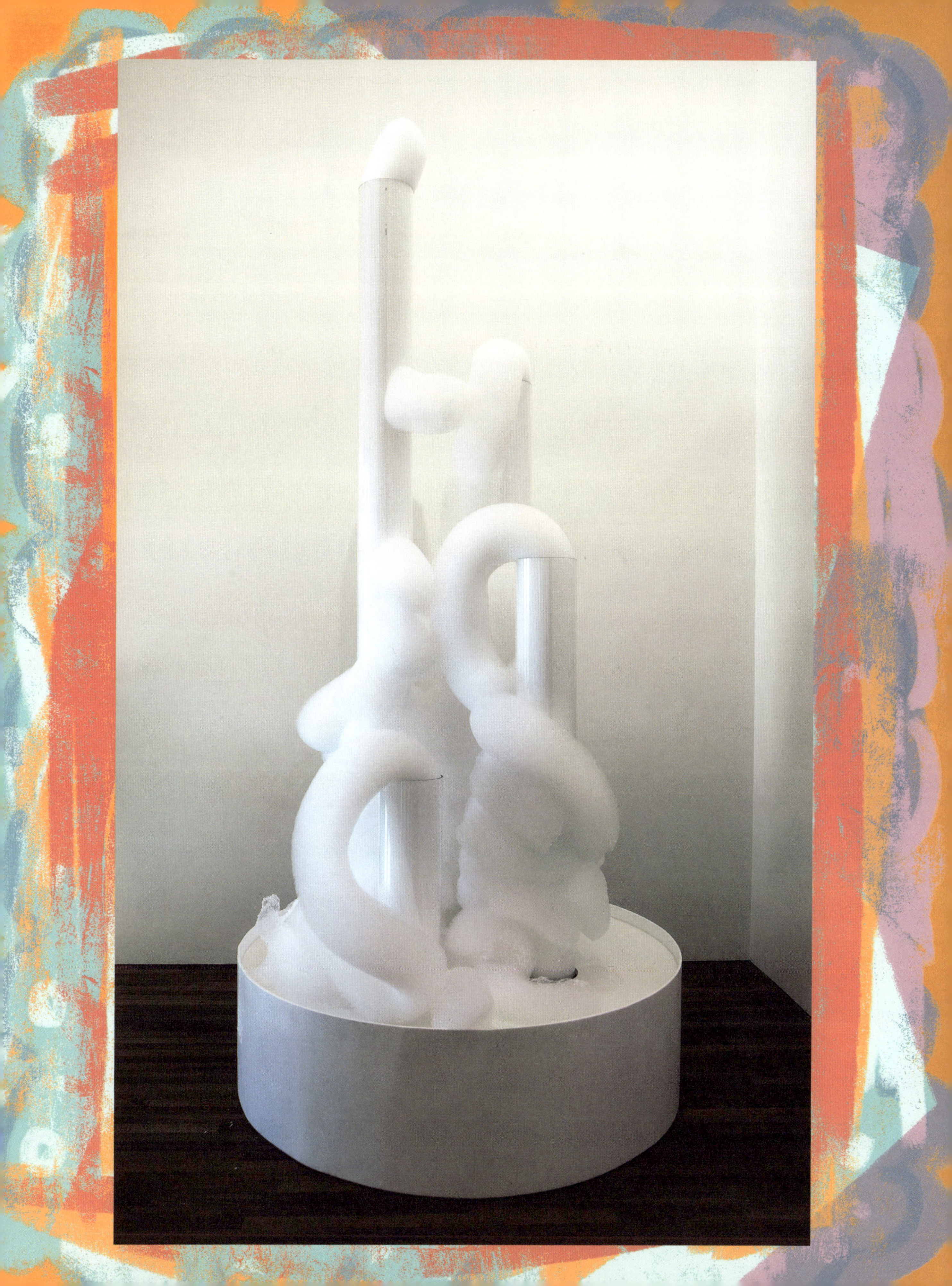

Bubbles form part of the dramatic images of Mr Medalla's childhood. He remembers watching his mother cook a dish of coconut and fruits for him when he was sick, and seeing the bubbles rise from the cauldron. Later, Mr Medalla would be fascinated by the bubbles he saw in a brewery in Edinburgh, Scotland.

MR MEDALLA'S CLOUDS ARE NEVER THE SAME SHAPE, SO THIS SCULPTURE LOOKS DIFFERENT AT EVERY MOMENT OF THE DAY!

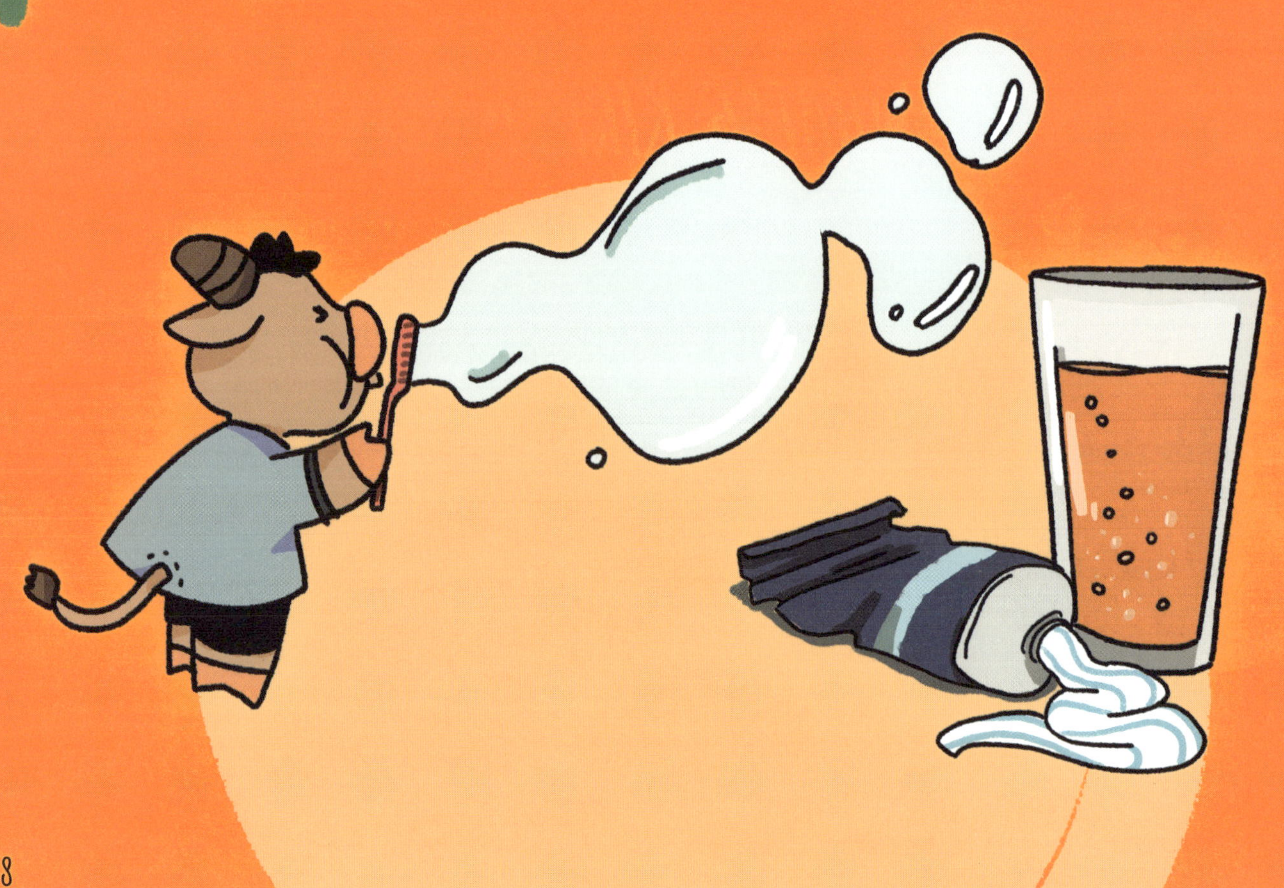

ABOUT THE ARTIST

David Medalla was born in the Philippines in 1942. He grew up near historic Manila Bay, where he often swam and played. Memories of those carefree days would later be a source of inspiration for his wide-ranging works, which include painting, sculpture and installation as well as kinetic and performance art.

According to Mr Medalla, he was only 12 when he moved to New York to study. Then, after a few years back in Manila, he went to live in the United Kingdom. Since then, he has lived and worked in Europe and the USA, exhibiting his works around the world. Despite the many years he has spent overseas, Mr Medalla says his roots are still in the Philippines.

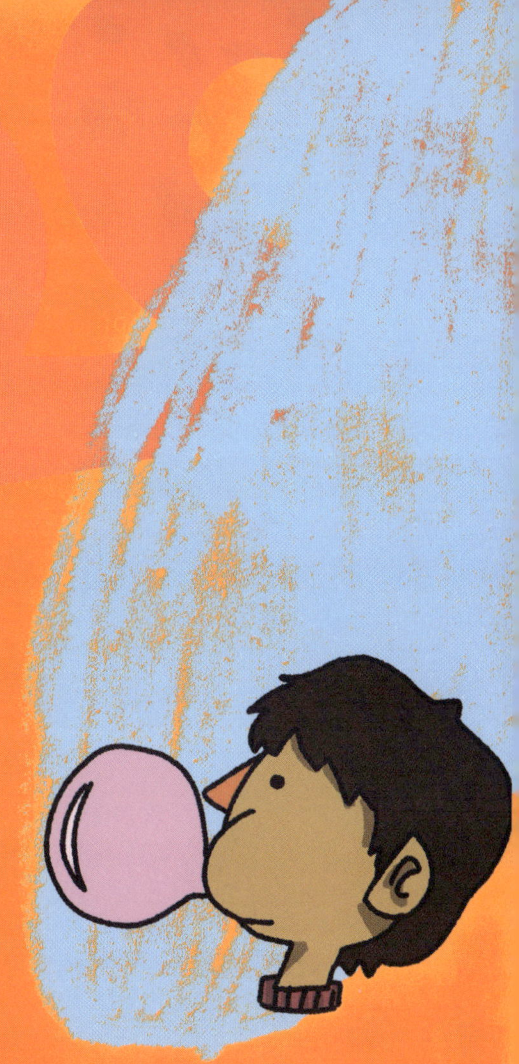

WHAT'S KINETIC ART?

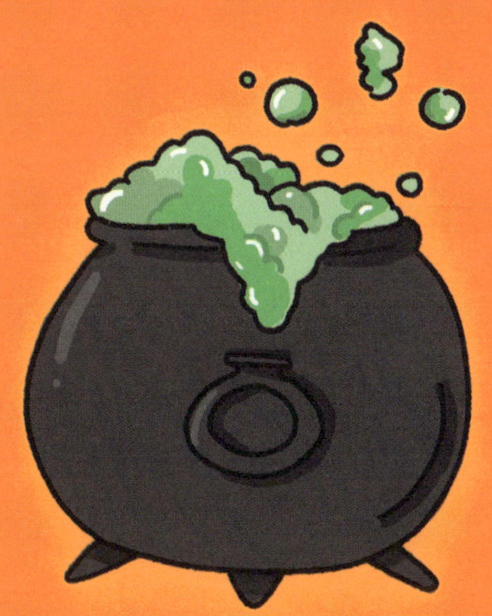

Unlike works of sculpture that are not meant to change, *Cloud Canyons No. 24* (2015) evolves in unpredictable ways because the movement of the bubbles cannot be controlled. Art that involves movement is known as kinetic art.

Movement in an installation can change its structure or the way it looks. Some artists create artworks powered by moving air. Other works may be set in motion by mechanical means, like *Cloud Canyons No. 24* (2015).

FUN WITH BUBBLES

Follow these steps to create your own bubble machine!

For this activity, you will need an empty plastic water bottle, a clean sock, rubber band, dish soap and water.

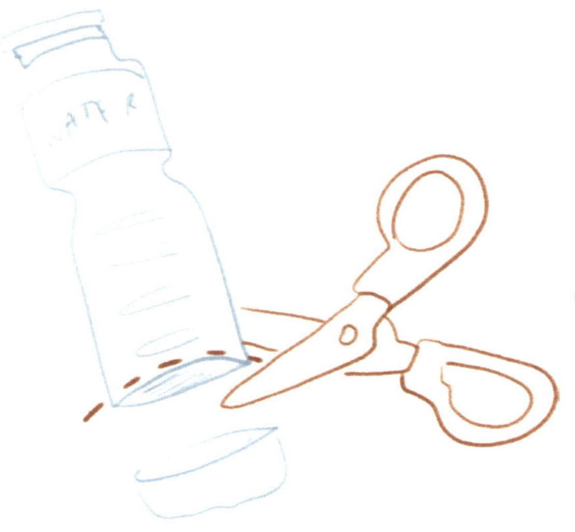

1

With a pair of scissors, carefully cut the bottom off the plastic bottle.

2

Stretch the clean sock over the cut end of the bottle. Secure the sock around the bottle with a rubber band. You have your bubble machine!

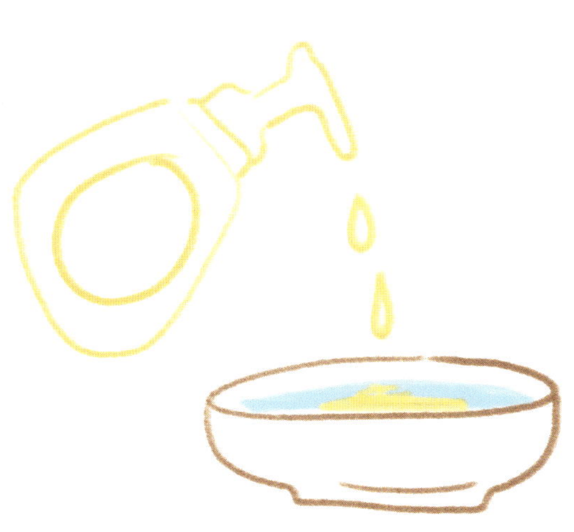

3

In a small bowl, mix 2 parts dish soap to 1 part of water.

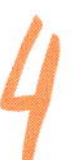

4

Dip the sock-end of your bubble machine into the mixture.

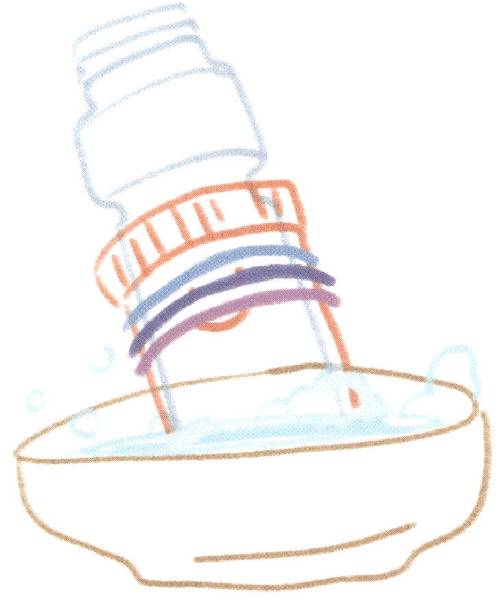

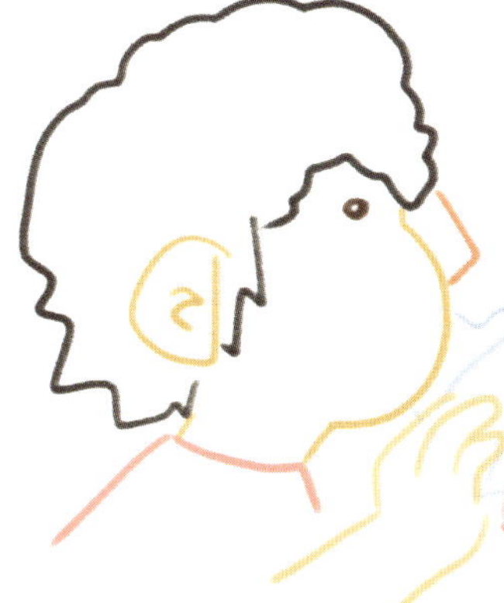

5

Blow into the other end of your bubble machine for bubbly fun!

What do your bubbles look like? How are you creating movement in your bubble machine? Can you think of other ways to make bubbles?

ONE LAST LOOK

The Philippines has such an array of visual arts. Take one last look at the works we've seen so far! We've seen paintings, sculptures and kinetic installations, but there's still so much to discover about the Philippines' visual arts.

You can visit many of these works yourself at the National Gallery Singapore. We hope you have enjoyed these stories and see you at the Gallery soon!

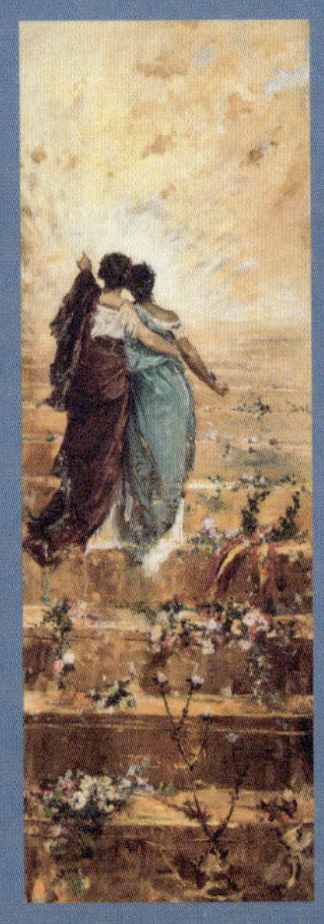

Juan Luna
España y Filipinas
(Spain and the Philippines)

1884
Oil on canvas,
299.5 x 79.5 cm

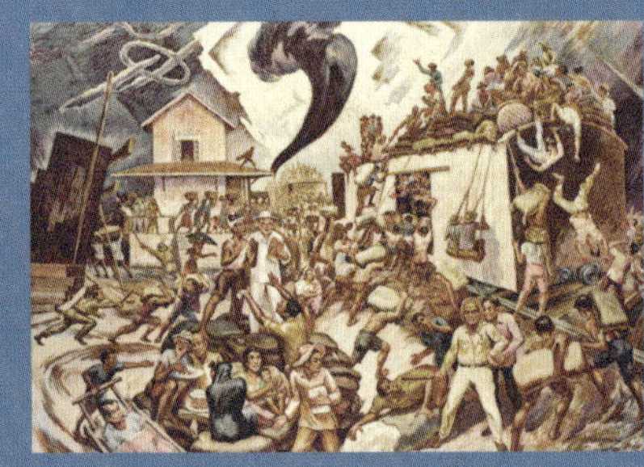

Ricarte Puruganan
Give Us This Day

c. 1974
Oil on canvas,
152.0 x 211.0 cm

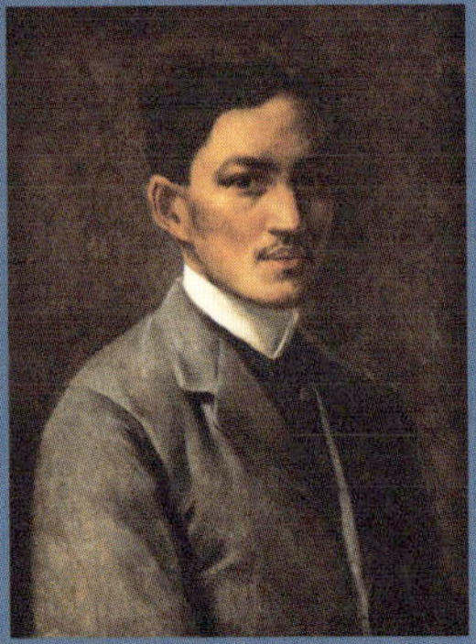

Fabian de la Rosa
Portrait of Jose Rizal

1902
Oil on canvas,
64.6 x 48.8 cm

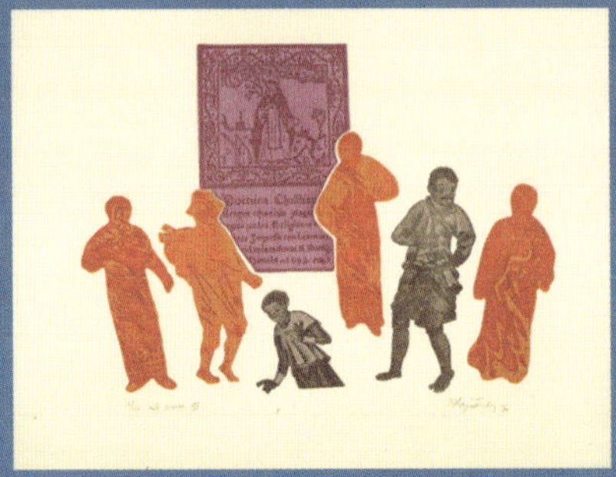

Imelda Cajipe-Endaya
Mga Ninuno VIII
(Ancestors VIII)

1979
Etching, aquatint, collagraphy and photoengraving on paper
Edition 25/25
37.5 x 50 cm

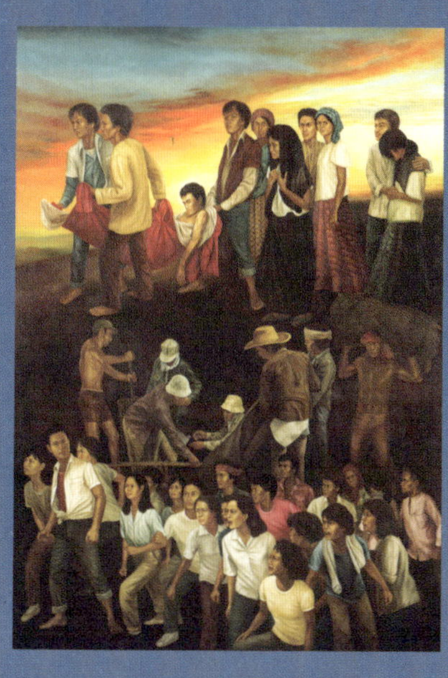

Renato Habulan
Dulang Bayan (A Nation's Drama)

1982
Oil on canvas,
213.4 x 152.4 cm
Image courtesy of Renato R. Habulan

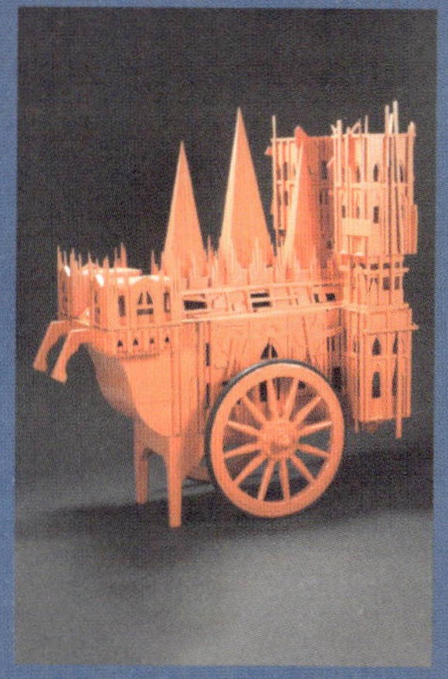

Jose Tence Ruiz
Paraisado Sorbetero (Orange)

2004
Mixed media (wood, iron, epoxy, rubber, polyester, resin, automotive enamel)
183 x 177 x 98 cm
Collection of Singapore Art Museum

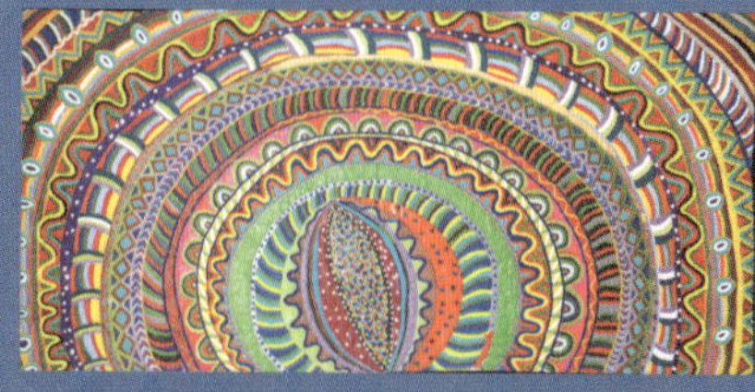

Pacita Abad
Evil Eye

1983
Acrylic, plastic buttons and ric rac ribbons on stitched and padded canvas,
132.5 x 263.5 cm
Gift of Jack and Kristiyani Garrity

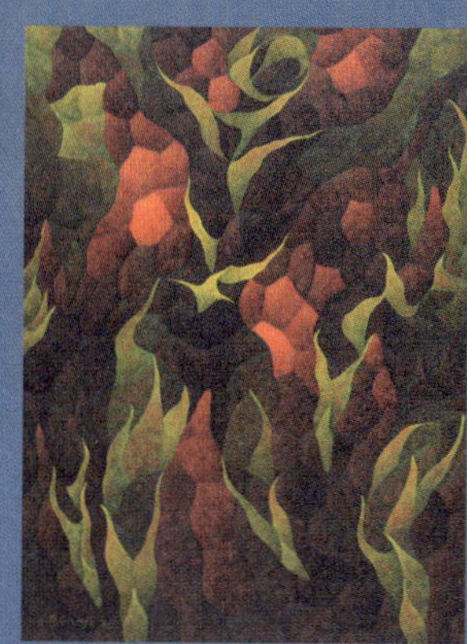

Hernando R. Ocampo
Dancing Mutants

1965
Oil on canvas,
101.8 x 76.0 cm

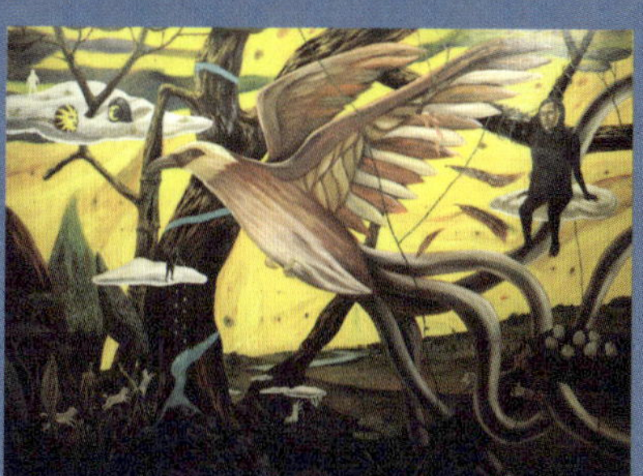

Rodel Tapaya
The Creation Myths

2009
Acrylic on canvas,
183.0 x 224.0 cm
Collection of Singapore Art Museum

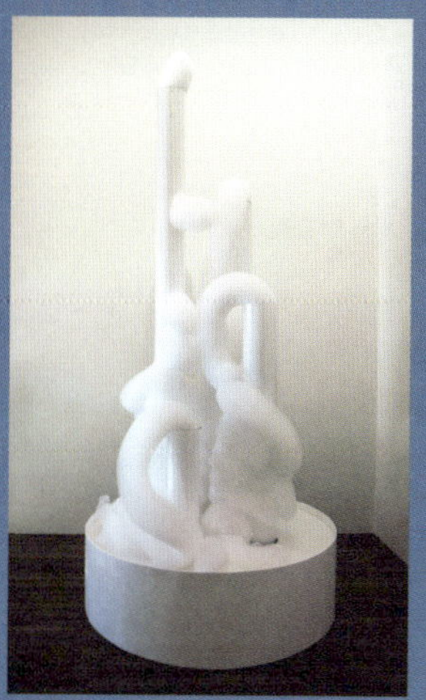

David Medalla
Cloud Canyons No. 24

2015, first version in series 1964
Wood, Perspex, compressors, timer, water and detergent,
310 x 150.0 x 150.0 cm

All artworks featured in this book are from the collection of the National Gallery Singapore, unless otherwise specified. All artwork images have been provided through the courtesy of the National Heritage Board, Singapore, unless otherwise mentioned.

Published 2020

Please direct all enquiries to the publisher at:
National Gallery Singapore
1 St Andrew's Road, #01-01
Singapore 178957

Author: Norma Olizon Chikiamco
Managing Editor: Elaine Ee
Project Editors: Joyce Choong and Sara Siew
Designer: Do Not Design
Illustrator: Sweet Gamboa

With kind assistance from:
the artists and their families, Clarissa Chikiamco, Phoebe Scott, Renée Staal and Tiara Izzanty

National Library Board, Singapore Cataloguing in Publication Data
Name(s): Olizon-Chikiamco, Norma.
Title: Awesome art Philippines : 10 works from the country of 7,000 islands everyone should know / by Norma O. Chikiamco. Other title(s): Awesome art.
Description: Singapore : National Gallery Singapore, 2020.
Identifier(s): OCN 1140023275 ISBN 978-981-14-2533-2 (paperback)
Subject(s): LCSH: Art, Philippine--Juvenile literature | Art, Philippine--Appreciation--Juvenile literature | Art appreciation--Juvenile literature.
Classification: DDC 709.599--dc23

CAN YOU SPOT THE PAIRS OF BIG ROUND EYES STARING AT YOU FROM THE COVERS OF THIS BOOK? THOSE BELONG TO PHILIPPINE TARSIERS! THEY ARE SMALL, NOCTURNAL ANIMALS THAT LIVE IN THE FORESTS OF SOUTHERN PHILIPPINES. LEARN MORE ABOUT THIS UNIQUE SPECIES BY LOOKING THEM UP ONLINE.

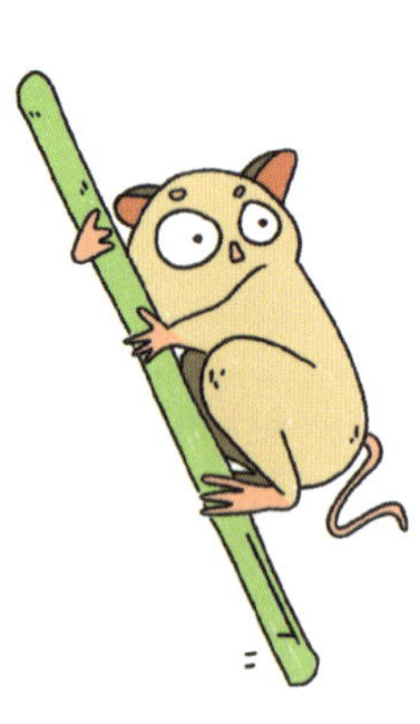